VACCINATIONS

From Smallpox to Cancer

VACCINATIONS

From Smallpox to Cancer

by Margaret O. Hyde and
Elizabeth H. Forsyth, M.D.

FRANKLIN WATTS
A Division of Grolier Publishing
New York • London • Toronto • Sydney
Danbury, Connecticut

615
Hyd

Acknowledgements

The authors thank Ben R. Forsyth, M.D., for his help.

Interior design by Molly Heron

Photographs©: AP/Wide World Photos: 103 (Gustavo Ferrari); Archive Photos: 19 (Kean Archives), 31; Corbis-Bettmann: 49 (Lester V. Bergman), 28 top, 30, 51, 60, 63 (UPI), 9, 10, 14, 26; Custom Medical Stock Photo: 21 (T.J. McDermott); Liaison Agency, Inc.: 33, 79 (Jean Marc Giboux), 12, 28 bottom, 54, 91, 106 (Hulton Getty), 36 (Ken Mengay), 77 (Sam Sargent); Peter Arnold Inc.: 83 (Ray Pfortner); Photo Researchers: 48 (Biophoto Associates), 71 (Maximilian Stock/SPL), 101 (Tom McHugh), 87 (Petit Format/C. Dauguet/C. Edelmann); PhotoEdit: 39 (Mary Steinbacher); Superstock, Inc.: cover, 93; Visuals Unlimited: 59 (Eric Anderson), 98 (Ken Greer), 45 (L. S. Stepanowicz).

Visit Franklin Watts on the Internet at:
http://publishing.grolier.com

Library of Congress Cataloging-in-Publication Data

Hyde, Margaret O. (Margaret Oldroyd), 1917–
    Vaccinations: from smallpox to cancer / Margaret O. Hyde and Elizabeth H. Forsyth.
    p. cm.
    Includes bibliographical references and index.
    Summary: An overview of vaccinations, explaining some basic terms, their development, with an emphasis on smallpox and polio vaccines, their current and future use, controversies concerning their use, and possible negative effects.
    ISBN 0-531-11746-4
    1. Vaccination—Juvenile literature. [1. Vaccination.] I. Forsyth, Elizabeth Held. II. Title.
RA638 .H93 2000
615'.372—dc21   99-045841

© 2000 Franklin Watts, a Division of Grolier Publishing Company
All rights reserved. Published simultaneously in Canada.
Printed in the United States of America.
1 2 3 4 5 6 7 8 9 10 R 09 08 07 06 05 04 03 02 01 00

Contents

1

Smallpox: A Success Story

SMALLPOX IS ONE disease you don't need a vaccination against. The *eradication* of smallpox, the complete removal of all traces of the disease, is the greatest triumph in the story of vaccination. The last naturally occurring outbreak of smallpox took place in 1977. Over the centuries, the microscopic particle, or virus, that causes smallpox probably killed more human beings than any other disease-causing organism.[1] Of course, no one knew about the existence of viruses in the days when smallpox occurred most often.

Smallpox, a serious contagious disease with long-lasting effects, spread from person to person in two ways—through contact and through breathing contaminated air. A healthy person could catch smallpox just by sitting next to an infected person. Infected people spread the virus by coughing and sneezing. The first symptoms were a high fever and chills. Then an angry rash developed, with hundreds of *pustules*—blisters or pimples filled with pus. Scabs formed on the pustules. When the scabs came off, scars remained.

People who survived smallpox had deep scars. The virus attacked their internal organs too, and their hands and feet swelled. Some people became deformed, and many lost their sight.[2] Young women who recovered from smallpox felt that the pockmarks that covered their faces and hands robbed them of their beauty. Indeed, smallpox could change a beautiful woman into an object of horror. The disease scarred infants and children for life.

Smallpox in the Past

Smallpox has a long history. It probably first appeared in China and the Far East about 3,000 years ago. Long before people had heard the word "vaccination," people in China tried to prevent the disease by exposing healthy individuals to pus from smallpox blisters. Perhaps they noticed that people who recovered from the disease did not get it again.

In 1175 B.C., the Egyptian pharaoh Ramses V died of smallpox. How do we know? Smallpox scars on the face of the mummified pharaoh are telltale signs. By the year 710, smallpox had reached Europe. Traders, travelers, and armies spread the disease over thousands of miles. In 1519, Spanish explorer Hernando Cortés carried smallpox to America. The sudden arrival of smallpox all but wiped out the Native Americans.[3]

The following description helps us picture the extent of illness and death caused by smallpox in the early sixteenth century. In the West Indies:

> . . . more than half the population died. . . in heaps like bedbugs. Many others died of starvation, because, as they were all taken sick at once, they could not care for each other, nor was there anyone to give them bread or anything else. In many places it happened that everyone in a house died, and, as it was impossible to bury the great number of dead, they pulled down the houses over them in order to check the stench that rose from the dead bodies, so that the houses became their tombs.[4]

In Europe, smallpox killed millions of people, and churchyards filled with corpses. People lived in constant fear of a disease that killed 40 percent of its victims.[5] In the eighteenth century,

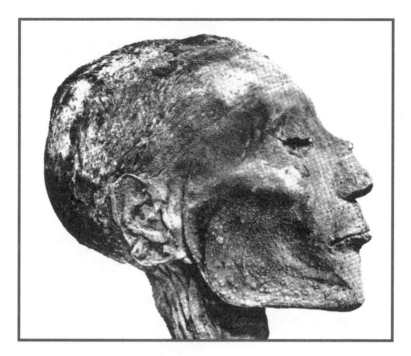

The mummified face of this Egyptian pharaoh shows clear traces of a horrible disease—probably smallpox.

called "the century of smallpox terror," fairs and markets were sometimes cancelled. In England, taverns advertised that they were well aired and free of the disease. A young person applying for a job as an apprentice had a better chance of finding one if he had recovered from smallpox. Otherwise, the apprentice might get the disease and pass it on to the master and his family. People knew for a fact that if the disease did not kill them, it would scar them for life.

Methods of Inoculation Against Smallpox

In the early eighteenth century, Lady Mary Wortley Montagu, wife of the British ambassador to Turkey, played an important role in the history of smallpox. Stricken with the disease at age 26, she recovered but was scarred for life. In Turkey, where she went with her husband, she saw people making powder from the scabs of smallpox pustules and placing the powder in other people's veins with the help of a needle. She watched one old woman open a vein in a person's arm, dip a needle into a nutshell filled with pus from a smallpox sore, and insert it into the other person's vein. The old woman repeated this action several times. This procedure, which seemed to protect thousands of Turks who had this treatment, impressed Lady Montagu so much that she ordered it for her young son.

Lady Mary Wortley Montagu, who lived from 1689 to 1762, played an important role in the history of smallpox.

When Lady Montagu returned to England, she did much to promote this method of infecting people with a small dose of smallpox to prevent them from developing a serious case. This technique, which became known as *variolation,* excited both doctors and patients. People no longer had to suffer the horrors of smallpox. This preventive method spread throughout Great Britain and Europe.

Several other methods of variolation were developed in the early 1700s. In one method, a needle was used to remove pus from a smallpox sore, and the pus was placed under the skin of an uninfected person with the same needle. Sometimes scabs were peeled from smallpox sufferers, dried, and ground into a powder that was inhaled by the person to be protected. In all these forms of *inoculation,* an individual received a weakened form of a disease to prevent the development of a more dangerous form.

After an *incubation period*—the time it takes for symptoms of disease to appear—the inoculated person usually suffered a mild attack of the disease and had a reasonable chance of survival. However, if the person lived through this first mild attack, there was a small chance of a second attack. Actually, inoculation increased the number of people who had mild cases of smallpox, and they spread it to those who could not afford inoculation. So a large number of poor people were exposed to the disease.[6]

Even though inoculation against smallpox sometimes caused sickness and death, many people believed it was worth the risk. In 1721 in Boston, during a smallpox *epidemic,* a physician named Zabdiel Boylston introduced the inoculation of smallpox into the American colonies at the request of Cotton Mather, a Puritan minister. At first, many other doctors opposed Boylston's actions, and he was attacked by angry mobs for ignoring a law against inoculation. But with fewer deaths from smallpox, inoculation increased in popularity. Compulsory inoculation began during the Revolutionary War, when General George Washington had his troops inoculated against smallpox.[7]

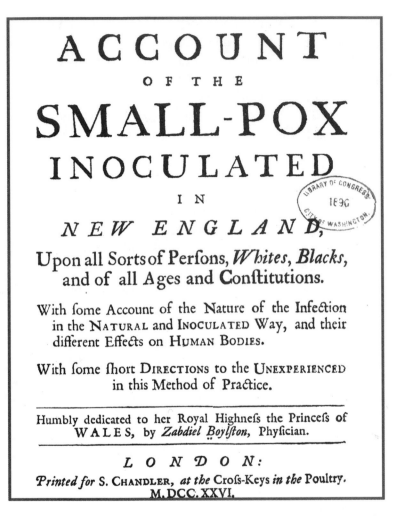

ACCOUNT

OF THE

SMALL-POX

INOCULATED

IN

NEW ENGLAND,

Upon all Sorts of Perſons, *Whites, Blacks,* and of all Ages and Conſtitutions.

With ſome Account of the Nature of the Infection in the NATURAL and INOCULATED Way, and their different Effects on HUMAN BODIES.

With ſome ſhort DIRECTIONS to the UNEXPERIENCED in this Method of Practice.

Humbly dedicated to her Royal Highneſs the Princeſs of WALES, by *Zabdiel Boylſton,* Phyſician.

LONDON:

Printed for S. CHANDLER, *at the* Croſs-Keys *in the* Poultry.
M.DCC.XXVI.

In the early 1700s, Zabdiel Boylston, an American physician, described the results of inoculation against smallpox.

The Development of Vaccination Against Smallpox

In the late 1700s, milkmaids in England were known for their beautiful skin—skin that was not scarred from smallpox. When milkmaids milked the cows, they often handled the udders of infected cows and were thus exposed to cowpox—a common infection in dairy cows. The milkmaids developed pustules that resembled smallpox on their hands. After they suffered a flulike illness, the scabs came off the pus-filled blisters, leaving only small scars. It was well known among many country people that a person who had developed cowpox would never catch smallpox. They had *immunity* to smallpox.

In 1774, an English farmer named Benjamin Jesty gave his wife and sons cowpox disease to protect them from smallpox. He used a cobbler's needle to transfer pus from a cow's udder to his family members. Jesty and his family became the object of the neighbors' ridicule, and some of them wondered if Jesty's family would turn into cows, or at least grow horns.[8] Although the London Medical Society knew of this experiment, its members paid little attention.

Several years later, the English doctor Edward Jenner took a different approach to preventing the horrible effects of smallpox. When he was a child, he had been inoculated against smallpox, and he had a lasting interest in how the disease was spread. Over a long period of time, he collected evidence showing that cowpox protected against smallpox. A detailed recording of his inquiry into the causes and effects of cowpox has been recently reprinted in the book *Vaccination Against Smallpox*.[9]

In May 1796, Jenner selected a healthy 8-year-old boy, named James Phipps, for a human experiment. He took some pus from a farmer's daughter who was infected with cowpox and put it in James's arm. Although the boy became ill the next day, he was well again the day after that. On July 1, 1796, Jenner scratched some human smallpox pus under the boy's skin—and he did not get sick.[10] According to at least one report, Jenner inoculated Phipps as many as 20 times and no smallpox appeared. Jenner had a cottage built for Phipps, who lived to enjoy his old age.[11]

No one had yet heard of the word "vaccination," which is based on *vacca,* the Latin word meaning "cow." Jenner had invented vaccination! He had proved that the relatively harmless

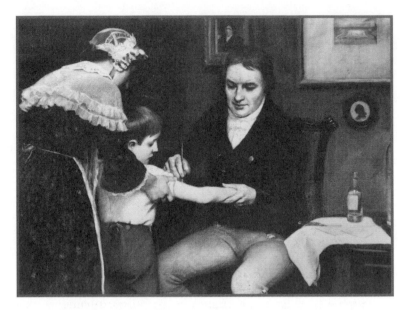

In England in 1796, Dr. Edward Jenner vaccinated 8-year-old James Phipps against smallpox.

cowpox disease could be used to immunize people against smallpox. By the end of the nineteenth century, the word "vaccination" was widely used and applied to protection against other diseases. Although not everyone accepted Jenner's idea that infection with cowpox could provide protection against smallpox, many people noted that vaccinations worked, and the number of them increased.

Jenner's experiment would not be permitted today. In Jenner's time, however, there were no committees on medical ethics that decided what was right and wrong. He did what was acceptable in his day.[12]

The Current Situation

Just 4 years after Jenner's experiment, smallpox vaccinations began in the United States, and by the beginning of the twentieth century, their use was widespread. In 1855, the state of Massachusetts passed a law requiring the vaccination of all school-children, and other states soon followed.[13] As the number of people who received vaccinations increased, the number of cases of smallpox decreased. The last documented case in the United States occurred in 1949, but most states continued to require smallpox vaccination for school admission until 1971—just in case someone brought smallpox into the United States from another country.[14]

In 1972, just two outbreaks of smallpox occurred in East Africa. In early 1974, an epidemic killed more than 25,000 people in India.[15] In 1977, the last naturally occurring smallpox outbreak took place in Somalia. The World Health Organization (WHO), which started an impressive campaign in 1967 that led to the eradication of smallpox in just 10 years, deserves much of the credit.

After smallpox was eradicated, stocks of smallpox virus were kept in laboratories in Russia and the United States, where the virus was frozen in liquid nitrogen for future research. The virus could be handled only by scientific workers wearing protective suits. By the late 1980s, only 600 tiny vials of smallpox virus remained in the two countries. However, North Korea and other countries are believed to have secret supplies of the smallpox virus.

Why are stocks of the smallpox virus still kept? Some experts have expressed concern that the virus may reappear naturally or that it may be used in an act of terrorism as a biological weapon. They believe that scientists are trying make the smallpox virus even more lethal than it already is. However, there are only 7 million doses of smallpox vaccine in the United States right now, and it would take several years to make enough to protect everyone. According to one estimate, an attack with a spray of smallpox that infected just 100 people would paralyze a large part of the country within a few weeks as it spread among unvaccinated individuals.[16]

At one time, the WHO recommended the destruction of all stocks of smallpox virus by June 30, 1999. In March 1999, however, a committee of the Institute of Medicine—a private, non-profit organization made up of top scientists who advise the federal government about medical care, research, and public health—reported that preserving the smallpox virus could bring about new and important discoveries that have real potential for improving human health. Research on the virus is providing new information on genes as well as on protein structure and function. Scientists who are making maps of the genetic information in the smallpox virus have found surprising links between genes in the virus and natural immune substances, including some involved in cancer.[17] The experts have agreed to reconsider the future of the remaining smallpox virus in June 2002.

Vaccination has wiped out smallpox throughout the world. Eradication of smallpox has meant that vaccination against smallpox is a thing of the past.

2

How Do Vaccinations Work?

SINCE THE DAYS when smallpox was epidemic, people have learned a lot about some diseases and why vaccinations work. We are surrounded by a sea of *microbes* that reproduce in large numbers, and your body is an ideal habitat for many of them. They invade through your skin and lungs—they are in the air you breathe. You swallow them along with your food and drink.

Vaccinations prevent you from getting some diseases caused by these tiny microbes. Vaccinations have benefited children more than any other preventive program in the world, with the possible exception of the purification of drinking water.[1] Vaccines have eradicated smallpox throughout the world, and they have wiped out polio in most countries. All children in the United States are safe from polio today. About 80 percent of U.S. children are also protected against such diseases as diphtheria, measles, whooping cough, and tetanus.

Today, more than forty vaccines prevent infection, disease, and person-to-person transmission. For example, without vaccination, polio would paralyze about 10,000 American children a year, and *rubella*—or German measles—would cause birth defects and mental retardation in about 20,000 newborns. Before vaccines were available, many thousands of children died or became deaf, blind, or brain-damaged due to diseases that are no longer common in the United States. The vaccination of children in developing countries is a goal for the twenty-first century.

Microbes and Immunization

In the late 1800s in France, Louis Pasteur demonstrated how microbes cause disease. He was working on chickens infected with cholera, a serious intestinal disease caused by bacteria, when he made an important discovery. He noticed that an old, weakened *culture* of the cholera bacteria that usually caused the disease did not make the chickens sick. When Pasteur tried to infect the same chickens with new, fresh cholera bacteria, he discovered that the old culture had made them immune to the disease-causing bacteria. Aging the bacteria had somehow made them less *virulent*, or toxic, and produced immunity.

Pasteur's experiment established a basic principle of immunization with vaccines.[2] *Attenuated*, or weakened, cultures of other serious infectious diseases such as *anthrax* and *rabies* could be used to prevent infections in animals in the laboratory. But would the method work in humans? Pasteur found the answer in a famous experiment.

In 1885, 9-year-old Joseph Meister was bitten by a dog who had rabies. Joseph's parents and Pasteur knew that the boy would die without help. At his parents' request, Pasteur injected the boy with a small dose of serum, the yellowish fluid from the blood of a rabbit that had died of rabies.

Pasteur had never used this serum on a human being before, and no one knew what the results of this treatment would be. When Joseph did not get rabies, Pasteur knew that his idea worked. People could be protected from a dangerous disease by the injection of a small amount of weakened serum.[3] This was the first attenuated vaccine.

The scientist Louis Pasteur developed and used vaccines that protect against rabies and anthrax.

The Immune System

Whenever the body senses the presence of a foreign substance such as a vaccine, it reacts and defends itself through a complex network of cells and organs known as the immune system. Two important characteristics of the immune system make it easier for us to understand it. One is the ability to tell the difference between "self"—the body's own healthy tissues—and "non-self"—foreign invaders, such as bacteria and viruses. Virtually every cell in the body has a distinctive marker that identifies it as "self." The other important characteristic of the immune system is its ability to remember previous invaders and react accordingly. For example, if you have had the measles, your immune system prevents you from getting it again.

All foreign organisms in the human body, whether they are beneficial or harmful, have special markers called *antigens.* Antigens that cause immune reactions in the body may be microbes such as a virus or even part of a virus. Tissues or cells from another person (except identical twins) carry "nonself" markers that act as antigens. As a result, the immune system of a person who has an organ transplant sometimes rejects the donor organ as foreign material. To minimize organ rejection, it is important to find a donor whose tissue is as similar as possible to that of the recipient. Transplant patients take drugs that help counteract the body's tendency to rid itself of foreign tissue.

The presence of foreign antigens causes the immune system to produce substances called *antibodies,* which are protein molecules that attack and destroy the invaders. Antibodies are formed to fight specific antigens. The immune system, which recognizes millions of different "nonself" molecules, produces specific molecules and cells to match up with each antigen and make it ineffective. Antibodies are formed in *lymph nodes,* where some immune cells gather, and in bone marrow, which is the tissue inside bones where blood cells are formed. The antibodies are released into the bloodstream to bind and neutralize antigens throughout the body.

Various kinds of cells make up the immune system. Each cell has a particular task. There is a special circulatory system, too, known as the lymphatic system, which is made up of the *lymphatic vessels* and the lymph nodes. The lymphatic vessels act in close partnership with the blood circulation and carry the *lymph,* a clear fluid that contains white blood cells.

The white blood cells that play the most important part in understanding how vaccines work are the *lymphocytes.* Nearly 1 trillion lymphocytes are transported to tissues throughout the

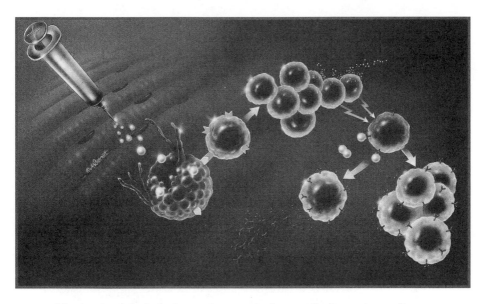

Vaccines work by inducing antigens to produce antibodies against a disease.

body, where they act as sentries—constantly on the lookout for foreign invaders.

The two main kinds of lymphocytes are the *B cells* and the *T cells*. B cells produce antibodies that circulate in the bloodstream and the lymphatic vessels, where they attach to foreign antigens to mark them for destruction by other immune cells. T cells have two main tasks. Some direct and regulate immune responses, and others are killer cells. The killer cells attack cells that are infected or cancerous. T cells also activate white blood cells known as *macrophages*—scavengers that gobble up debris. The word "macrophage" comes from a Greek word meaning "big eater."[4]

Types of Immunity

Whenever the body uses B cells and T cells, some of them become *memory cells*. Although the other antibodies used to destroy an infectious agent do not remain, the memory cells stick around. As long ago as the fifth century B.C., Greek physicians noted that people who recovered from the plague, a severe bacterial disease, did not get it again. Now we know that some of the cells in people's immune systems become memory cells, so when they encounter an invader that they have met before, they recognize it and destroy it.

Suppose you have had chickenpox, for example. The next time you are exposed to the disease, the memory cells recognize the invader, and the immune system quickly mounts its defense. Your immune system knocks out the invader before you ever feel ill. Because you have already had chickenpox, you have *active immunity* to the disease. You acquire natural active immunity by getting a disease and artificial active immunity when you are vaccinated against a disease.

Or suppose the boy sitting next to you has the flu. If you have been vaccinated against the strain of flu that reaches your body when he sneezes, your immune system is ready to respond. If you are exposed to flu virus after being vaccinated, the microbes stimulate a system that is already primed to fight them. Memory cells are also involved in the other diseases for which you have received vaccinations.

When you get antibodies produced by another animal or human, you have *passive immunity*. You were born with some natural passive immunity, which your mother gave you. Sometimes people are vaccinated to give them artificial passive immunity. These people need to be protected when they are particularly vulnerable to a disease—for example, immediately after exposure to a serious illness.

To better understand artificial passive immunity, consider this. Larry had the measles in the days before there was a vaccine for the disease. He had just recovered from it when his family was scheduled to leave for a cruise. His brother, Bruce, had never had measles, so there was a good chance that Bruce would come down with the disease during the cruise. To prevent this from happening, the doctor gave Bruce injections of *gamma globulin*—the part of the blood that contains a large concentration of antibodies. This kind of immunization becomes effective quickly, but it does not last long.

People get artificial active immunity through vaccination. Vaccines do not cause disease, but they can stimulate the immune system, thus causing active immunity. If Bruce had been vaccinated against measles, he would not have needed gamma globulin. His own immune system would have been able to fight off the disease.

Types of Vaccines

Inactivated vaccines are made of killed bacteria or viruses that have been inactivated by chemicals or heat. These vaccines are safe and stable, and they cannot cause disease. However, they stimulate a relatively weak response from the immune system, so people usually need several *booster* shots. The flu shot is an inactivated vaccine.

Live attenuated vaccines are made from live but weakened microbes. The vaccines for measles, German measles, and mumps are made from live attenuated organisms. The microbes are weakened by growing them under special conditions in tissue cultures in the laboratory. Because these vaccines stimulate the immune system more strongly, people usually need only one booster. Most of these vaccines are injected, but some, such as the Sabin polio vaccine, can be given by mouth.

Very rarely, the weakened microbes in a live vaccine can change to a virulent form that can cause disease. As a precaution, doctors do not give live vaccines to pregnant women or people with damaged immune systems, such as those with human immunodeficiency virus (HIV) or cancer or those who take medicines that suppress their immune systems. Your doctor can tell you if you should avoid having a certain vaccination.

Many microbes that infect people are not harmful themselves, but they produce toxins—very powerful poisons that cause illness. Vaccines that protect against toxins must be made from inactivated toxins, called *toxoids*. Chemicals are used to inactivate the toxins so that they are harmless but still capable of stimulating antibodies. Toxoids are used to immunize people against diphtheria and tetanus. After you receive a vaccination against tetanus, you develop antibodies to the toxoids or *antitoxins*.

We have vaccines to protect us against diseases such as smallpox, polio, measles, mumps, chickenpox, and flu. But as yet, there is no vaccine against acquired immunodeficiency syndrome, better known as AIDS. What about cancer? Some experimental vaccines against cancer are being tested. Immunologists are searching for certain antigens on the surfaces of cancer cells in their efforts to produce cancer vaccines.[5] You will find out more about the search for effective cancer vaccines in Chapter 9.

3

Polio: Moving Toward Success

POLIO SHOULD BE the next disease after smallpox to be eradicated worldwide. By 1999, children in the Western world, including those in the United States, as well as children in East Asia and the Pacific Basin were free from polio.[1] Like smallpox, polio affects only humans, making eradication possible.

Polio, which is caused by a virus, can strike quickly. The microbe enters the mouth or nose and travels through the body into the intestines, where it multiplies. After the virus multiplies in the intestines, it goes into the bloodstream, where people make antibodies against it. Once in the blood, the poliovirus may enter the nervous system, where it destroys the nerves that control muscle movements and may cause paralysis.

A few days after infection, some people have no symptoms at all. People with mild cases of polio have flulike symptoms, such as headache, nausea, diarrhea, and fever. Those with more severe disease may have varying amounts of paralysis. People can spread polio to others for as long as 2 weeks after infection, whether or not they show symptoms. The number of infected people who develop polio symptoms may be as low as 10 percent, and as few as 1 percent develop paralysis.[2] Other people are luckier. Their bodies make antibodies that stop the progression of the disease.

Even in a world without new cases of polio, many of the 1.6 million survivors of the disease suffer from a condition known as postpolio syndrome. This condition can strike from 10 to 50 years after the original attack. Some of the symptoms include unusual fatigue, new weakness in muscles (whether or not they were originally affected), pain in muscles and joints, muscle spasms, and breathing difficulties.

Polio in the Past

For centuries, polio probably caused death and paralysis. Some historians believe evidence of the disease is preserved on an Egyptian stone engraving more than 3,000 years old.[3] There may

In this Egyptian stone engraving, the front foot of the person on the left has probably been deformed by polio.

have been some scattered cases in the eighteenth century, too, but no one knows for sure. Over the next hundred years, small epidemics were reported in a number of countries.[4]

When people tossed the contents of chamber pots out of windows and open sewers ran down the streets, polio infected each new generation of infants. Most of them did not get sick, because their mothers' antibodies gave them some protection. Infants may have suffered mild cases of polio, with symptoms no worse than a cold, and rarely received diagnoses of polio. Even a mild case of polio protected people against the disease for the rest of their lives.[5]

Strange as it may seem, the number of polio cases increased when sanitation improved. With better hygiene, there was less chance for infants and children to get the mild form of polio and acquire immunity. When the disease struck older children or adults, it was more likely to paralyze them.

Fear of Polio

People in the United States did not feel the full impact of polio until 1916, when an epidemic caused widespread panic.[6] Throughout the summers of the next few decades, fear of the disease caused people to flee from the cities to the mountains and stay away from crowds and bathing beaches. Movie theaters closed, meetings were canceled, and public gatherings were avoided. Doctors postponed minor operations for children until the weather was cooler.

In the 1940s and 1950s, the great polio epidemic that swept through the United States left about 640,000 children with various degrees of paralysis.[7] The poliovirus killed many children and left thousands suffering from paralysis that ranged from mild to extreme. Parents everywhere lived in fear of "infantile paralysis."

Polio was a dread disease. It was especially frightening because it could cripple arms and legs, leaving children in braces and wheelchairs. Children who suffered paralysis of the muscles involved in breathing were placed in a device called an iron lung,

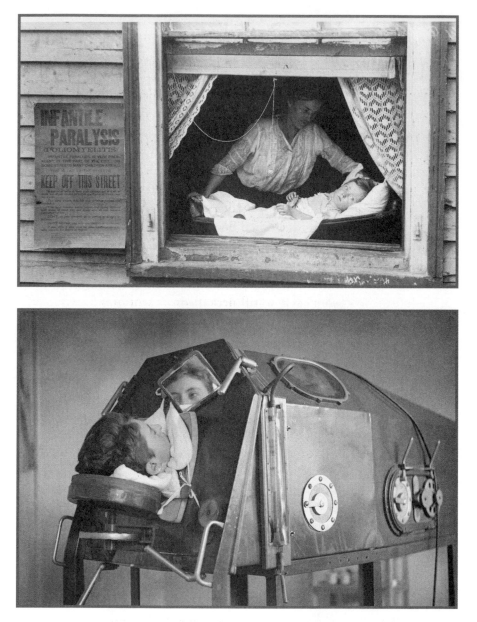

Polio, or infantile paralysis, affected many young children. Notices warned people to keep away from the sick children (top). Doctors put this young polio patient in an iron lung. A mirror located near the child's head helped him to see what was going on in the room (bottom).

which took over the work of the useless muscles so that the lungs could take in air. An iron lung looked something like a horizontal space capsule with the child's head poking out at one end.

In the summer of 1952, your parents would probably have told you not to swim in public pools or the ocean for fear you would get polio. Parents and doctors watched for the disease everywhere. People even allowed their fear of polio to interfere with medical treatment in an emergency situation. A true story illustrates this point.

Four-year-old Ben was having fun at the beach, jumping over piles of sand, until he felt a sudden, terrible pain in his side. At the hospital, doctors diagnosed Ben's problem as a hernia, a condition in which a loop of the intestines gets pinched in a weakened part of the muscular wall of the belly. An emergency operation was scheduled to repair it. But when Ben developed a fever and complained of a stiff neck, doctors sent him home to wait until they were sure he did not have polio. If Ben had polio, he had to be isolated.

Authorities reported the occurence of more than 50,000 cases of polio in the summer of 1952, but Ben was not one of them. He may have had a mild case of the disease. When his temperature returned to normal, he went back to the hospital. A surgeon repaired his hernia, and Ben grew up without suffering any lasting effects from polio.

Polio Vaccines

Although there is still no cure for polio, the disease is now preventable due to the development of vaccines. Work on these vaccines began in the early 1900s, but these attempts failed. Research about polio grew through painstaking efforts, much of which was funded by the March of Dimes. President Franklin D. Roosevelt, who was crippled with polio before he became president, helped found this organization. He declared a war on polio during his administration, and tremendous resources became available to support the search for a vaccine to prevent the disease.

Franklin D. Roosevelt, the thirty-second president of the United States, developed polio when he was an adult.

In 1947, Dr. Jonas Salk, who was working in the field of vaccine development, began his research on polio. He found a way to process the three strains of viruses that cause polio so that they were weaker. In 1953, he succeeded in developing an effective vaccine using a mixture of all three types of the poliovirus grown in monkey kidney cultures. By using the chemical formalin, he killed the whole viruses.[8] The proteins of the destroyed virus "taught" the immune system of vaccinated individuals to recognize the poliovirus and gave people immunity to the disease.

The results of a large trial of the Salk vaccine in children in the United States and Canada showed a dramatic reduction of illness in the vaccinated group, and in 1955, the government gave permission for the vaccine to be used for all children. People hailed Dr. Salk as a miracle worker. When he refused to *patent* the vaccine he had developed, his popularity increased. He said he did not want to make money from the vaccine. He wished only to see it used in as many places as possible.[9]

Dr. Jonas Salk (right), who developed the first vaccine against polio, and Dr. Albert B. Sabin (left), who developed the oral vaccine against the disease, attended the Third International Polio Congress in Rome.

The Salk vaccine gives lasting—but not always lifelong—immunity against polio, and people can still spread the disease. To solve this problem, Albert Bruce Sabin began testing another form of polio vaccine in 1957. The Sabin vaccine contains live attenuated viruses for each of the three polio strains. The weakened virus induces immunity, but in rare cases—one in 750,000—it can cause paralytic polio. Because the injected Salk vaccine uses dead virus, the risk is less—only 1 in 2.4 million. The Sabin vaccine is given orally, often in sugar cubes, so it costs less, and trained medical workers are not needed to give shots.

Eradication of Polio

In 1988, the WHO set a target date for the eradication of polio from the world—the year 2000. When that goal was set, there were about 35,000 cases of polio reported worldwide. Over the next 8 years, that number declined by 90 percent.[10] Many organizations, such as Rotary International, along with some government workers and volunteers, helped with the campaign to fight the disease. Rotary groups played a major role in providing polio vaccine for immunization campaigns in the Philippines, Haiti, Bolivia, Morocco, Sierra Leone, and Gambia. In 1997, Rotary members helped mobilize some 150,000 volunteers to transport polio vaccine, and they also assisted doctors, health workers, and other nongovernmental organizations in remote areas in India.

The last case of "wild" polio—one that was caused by a naturally occurring virus—in the United States was reported in 1979, compared with more than 50,000 cases reported in 1952.[11] If polio is eradicated, the poliovirus may exist only in laboratory freezers, like smallpox.[12]

Although polio may join smallpox in the history books, the eradication of polio has not been without tragedy. Since "wild" polio was eliminated, about eight or nine cases of polio caused by oral vaccine have been reported each year in the United States.

At a polio immunization rally in Nepal, the international fight against polio continues.

Some cases have occurred in children who were vaccinated. Others, called contact cases, are the children, relatives, and caretakers of children who received oral vaccinations and then transmitted polio by "shedding" (releasing) the live virus in their body wastes.

To make vaccination against polio safer, in 2000 the Advisory Committee for Immunization Practices of the Centers for Disease Control and Prevention (CDC) began recommending vaccinating children in the United States with the inactivated virus only. The oral vaccine will no longer be given to people in the United States. The success of international polio eradication efforts means that the risk from oral vaccines is now greater than the risk posed by the disease.[13]

With no new cases of polio, the question remains: Should people still be vaccinated? Smallpox vaccination has ended, but should polio vaccination end too? Many experts think such a step would be foolish. Stocks of polio virus are now available globally, and there are concerns about accidental release, as well as the use of the virus by terrorists. This issue may loom large in the near future. But the polio story has a good ending for most people. Thanks to vaccines, children growing up today know polio only as a shot or a sugar cube. People who lived at the time of the epidemics, however, will not forget the crutches, wheelchairs, and iron lungs.

4

Trying to Control the Hepatitis ABCs

TANYA, WHO HAS just received a vaccination against hepatitis B, thinks she can never get *hepatitis*. She does not realize that there is more than one form of the disease. Hepatitis A, B, and C are the most common, but hepatitis D, E, F, and G also occur. Today, there are so many kinds of hepatitis that it has been called the "alphabet disease." Tanya's cousin once had hepatitis—actually, hepatitis A—probably from eating raw oysters from contaminated water. Tanya's vaccination for hepatitis B does not protect her from the other forms of hepatitis.

In the United States, about 33 percent of cases of hepatitis are hepatitis A, about 20 percent are hepatitis C, and a large percent of the remaining 47 percent are hepatitis B. About four times as many people may have hepatitis C as have HIV, the virus that causes AIDS.[1]

Hepatitis means "inflammation of the liver." The disease may be the result of alcohol or drugs, but viruses cause most hepatitis. People with viral hepatitis may have mild flulike symptoms, fatigue, loss of appetite, nausea, stomach pains, and diarrhea, followed by jaundice (yellowing of the skin or eyes). Because there is no effective treatment for hepatitis, prevention is important.

Hepatitis A

Hepatitis A is a disabling disease, but it is rarely fatal or chronic. Although it occurs much less often in the United States than in many other countries, it causes about 200,000 cases of illness in the United States every year.

How do you get hepatitis A? The virus is transmitted mainly by eating food or drinking water that has been contaminated with body wastes and by poor personal hygiene. Shellfish, such as oysters, mussels, lobsters, crabs, and clams, concentrate the virus when it is present in the water they live in. Shellfish get their

Shellfish may be a source of hepatitis A.

food by filtering hundreds of gallons of water through their bodies each day, and if the virus that causes hepatitis A is in the water, some of it remains in their bodies. You may see notices at some docks in the United States that warn people not to eat the shellfish from water in that area.

Hepatitis A is also spread by the transfer of body fluids. This can happen when using contaminated needles, but it is rare. The virus can survive at room temperature in contaminated diapers or on hands that are not washed after handling infected material. It can be a problem in day-care centers if workers do not wear disposable gloves when changing diapers or do not wash their hands after using the bathroom. Toddlers can spread the virus too. Young children are the source of half the cases of hepatitis A in the United States.[2] Children belong to one of the highest risk groups.[3] Food handlers in restaurants also spread the disease.

In October 1999, the CDC recommended routine vaccination of children against hepatitis A in areas where the disease is most common. The goal is eventual immunization for everyone. Vaccination is also recommended for travelers to all countries except Japan, Australia, New Zealand, and Canada. The vaccine can be given in two doses, at least 6 months apart, and may be given at the same time as other vaccines.

Hepatitis B

Hepatitis B, a more serious disease than hepatitis A, accounts for an estimated 4,000 to 5,000 deaths each year in the United States. Each year, an estimated 200,000 new infections occur, about 11,000 people are hospitalized, and 20,000 remain chronically infected. Overall, somewhere between 1 million and 1.25 million people in the United States are chronically infected with hepatitis B.[4] These people are known as chronic carriers—they have the disease for life. Even if they have no symptoms of hepatitis B, they can spread it to others. They are 200 times more likely to develop liver cancer than people who do not have hepatitis B.

Hepatitis B is very contagious—100 times more contagious than HIV. The virus that causes hepatitis B is spread primarily by contact with the blood or body fluids of an infected person as well as by sexual intercourse. An infected mother can easily pass the disease to her infant while giving birth. Unsterile needles used for ear piercing, body piercing, tattooing, administering drugs, and glucose testing also spread the disease. Sharing toothbrushes, razors, and washcloths can also transmit hepatitis B. Open sores, saliva, and breast milk are other sources of infection. Like the hepatitis A virus, the hepatitis B virus may be present on contaminated beaches and in shellfish, but becoming infected with hepatitis B by ingesting the virus is not common. However, in one case, drinking from the same can of soda pop spread hepatitis B.[5] In about one-third of the cases, the route of transmission is unclear.

Like hepatitis A, hepatitis B can cause fatigue, loss of appetite, pains in the joints or stomach, and diarrhea or vomiting. However, some people have no symptoms until serious liver damage has occurred. This happened to Arkesha Johnson, a healthy, active 15-year-old girl who lived in North Minneapolis, Minnesota. When she developed stomach pains and began vomiting, her mother took her to a local medical center. After some tests, the girl was taken to the hospital. She never went home again. Although she was at the top of the list for a liver transplant, her liver was so badly damaged that she died before a transplant was available—2 weeks after being diagnosed with hepatitis B.[6]

Such sudden death from hepatitis B is rare, but the disease can be very serious. Minnesota, where Arkesha Johnson died, was the first state to recommend that all teenagers be immunized against the hepatitis B virus. Since then, some states have required hepatitis B vaccination before entering seventh grade.

Today, large-scale immunization programs that include hepatitis B vaccination of infants are being carried out for two reasons. One, no one can predict which children will eventually become high-risk teenagers, who may be likely to develop the disease. Two, vaccination programs in infants are more effective than those for teenagers and adults.[7] Because hepatitis B sometimes leads to liver cancer, the vaccine helps prevent deaths from this form of cancer. Widespread childhood hepatitis B vaccinations seem wrong to some people, because children are not usually exposed to an exchange of blood and body fluids. Because antibiotics cannot cure hepatitis B, some experts say that prevention is the best option, especially because children infected before they are 6 years old have a much higher likelihood of developing liver cancer.[8]

Experience has shown that the vaccine for hepatitis B is very safe, and the medical, scientific, and public health communities strongly approve of it.[9] Hepatitis B vaccine has been recommended for everyone 18 years of age and younger, and for any adult over 18 who is at risk.[10] Today, infants receive hepatitis B shots along with their other immunizations. By

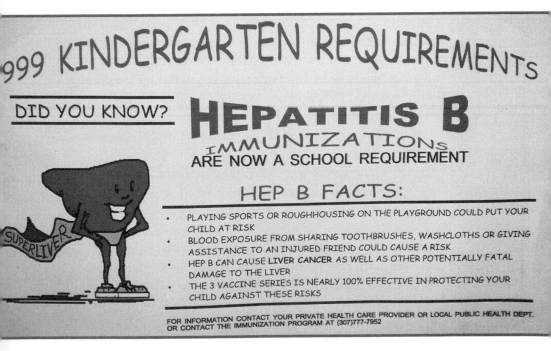

You may have been vaccinated against hepatitis B.

1998, 22 states required it for enrollment in kindergarten or first grade. However, many young people missed being immunized because they received their other immunizations before the vaccine became available. The American College Health Association urges vaccination against hepatitis B for all college students.

Hepatitis C

Most people who have hepatitis C do not know they are carrying the disease. For example, 30 years after Austin experimented with drugs in the 1960s, he learned that he was infected with hepatitis C. Austin suspected that the hepatitis C came from the dirty needles he used. At first he was very alarmed, but later he learned that 80 percent of infected individuals survive with no lasting effects of disease.[11] Not everyone is so lucky.

In cases of hepatitis C, doctors most often suspect that the cause was blood transfusions (before blood was screened for the virus), drug use, or unprotected sexual intercourse, but anything that spreads blood or body fluids may account for this infection. Joshua discovered he had hepatitis C when a routine blood test showed that his liver was not functioning properly. Like 10 percent of people with hepatitis C, Joshua does not know how he became infected.

In 1999, the Department of Veterans Affairs announced a screening program for hepatitis C to monitor how the disease progresses and to offer the newest treatment. Up to 20 percent of Vietnam veterans may be infected with hepatitis C.[12]

Treatment of hepatitis C is very expensive, and even when it works, side effects can be serious. People who have been exposed to the disease should tell their doctors and avoid drinking alcohol because it speeds up the liver damage caused by infection. Prevention of hepatitis C includes many of the guidelines recommended in the prevention of AIDS—halting the transfer of blood and body fluids. At present, no vaccine exists. The many variations among hepatitis C viruses make it difficult to develop a vaccine.

Prevention is important. By avoiding risky behavior, which involves the transfer of blood and body fluids, and getting immunized against hepatitis A and B, you can work to prevent these diseases.

5

What Vaccinations Have You Had?

BEFORE SHE WAS adopted, Kaitlyn lived with five different foster mothers. No one kept a record of her vaccinations, so her new doctor has insisted that she be vaccinated against all the usual childhood diseases. Kaitlyn thought that was ridiculous until one of her friends had a severe case of chickenpox that developed into pneumonia.

Kaitlyn is just one of many people who are not aware of the importance of vaccinations that protect people against serious diseases. A growing attitude among young parents that vaccinations are not necessary concerns many health experts. If not enough people are protected by vaccination, new outbreaks could occur. Many people have records of their vaccinations at home and at their doctor's office, but this is not always the case. Do you know which vaccines you were given when you were very young? Do you know which you should have in later years? Read this chapter and find out.

Diphtheria, Tetanus, and Pertussis (DTP and DTaP) Vaccines

Relatively few people alive today remember the tragedy of diphtheria, an infectious disease that is caused by bacteria. One woman, now a grandmother, had this disease when she was a child. She had a terribly sore throat and had trouble breathing. Her hair fell out too. She had diphtheria in 1920, along with many other people—about 148,000 of them died of the disease. Before a vaccine against diphtheria became available, about 15,000 people in the United States died of diphtheria every year.

Diphtheria occurred in much of the world before large numbers of people in North America and Europe received immunizations.[1] About half of the people who suffered from diphtheria died because there was no treatment. The bacteria enter the body through the nose and mouth and settle in the tonsils and throat, where they form a thick, gray, leathery membrane that can block the airway. Death from suffocation may result. The bacteria also produce a toxin that is carried in the bloodstream and causes severe damage to the heart and nervous system. This damage is responsible for most of the deaths.

Although antibiotics can destroy the diphtheria bacteria in the throat, passive immunization with antitoxin, which acts quickly, is needed to neutralize the toxin. To prevent damage, antitoxin must be given before the toxin binds to the body's tissue. People with diphtheria may seem to get better in the first few weeks after the disease first strikes, but the toxin may cause heart failure as long as 6 weeks after the start of the disease. Damage to the nervous system can cause paralysis that affects the ability to swallow and breathe, as well as weakness of the arms or legs.

Routine immunization of infants and children has almost eliminated death from diphtheria in the United States.[2] However, not everyone is protected from the disease. A 1996 survey in Minnesota reported that 62 percent of people from 18 to 39 years of age lacked adequate protection against diphtheria. Although no diphtheria epidemics occur now in the United States, the disease has reemerged in the countries of the former Soviet Union, where about 50,000 cases were reported in 1995.[3] Crumbling public health services and pressure from people who are against vaccinations have played a part in the return of this disease, killing 1,700 people.[4] Public health workers are on alert when there is a reintroduction of a serious disease because of the threat to the rest of the world. In the United States, booster doses of diphtheria vaccine are recommended at 10-year intervals along with the vaccine against tetanus.

Today, there are few cases of tetanus in the United States, but many occur in developing countries. Three days after an African boy named Yusif stepped on a sharp piece of glass that was sticking out of the soil in his native Sudan, he developed terrible symptoms. He had a severe headache, his heart beat rapidly, and the muscles all over his body became stiff. He could not control the severe painful muscle spasms. The contractions of his face and jaw muscles gave him a grotesque, grinning expression. Yusif was suffering from tetanus, which is commonly called "lockjaw" due to the stiffness of the jaw muscles. Spasms of the throat and chest muscles may interfere with breathing and cause death from suffocation.

Yusif soon died. A tetanus vaccination would have prevented his death, but in the Sudan and many other developing countries, infants are not always immunized against tetanus. This disease is one of the most common causes of newborn deaths in these countries, where infants are born under unsterile conditions to mothers who are not immunized. It is often customary to wrap the umbilical cord with soil.

Tetanus bacteria are found everywhere, but they are not dangerous in places where there is plenty of oxygen. If you get a puncture wound such as a deep cut or a cat bite, tetanus spores present in the soil or in animal feces can enter your body. Even careful washing does not ensure protection against tetanus toxin. Contrary to popular belief, it is not a rusty nail that causes tetanus, it is the spores on the nail. Because the spores are deprived of oxygen deep in a puncture wound, they change and produce toxin that quickly finds its way into the nervous system. This triggers the severe muscle spasms that Yusif had. In the United States, most cases of tetanus occur either in addicts who use injectable drugs or in burn victims whose skin provides a favorable place for growth of the tetanus bacteria.

This child is risking a tetanus infection by stepping on boards that may contain a nail and could puncture a foot. This could introduce tetanus spores.

Even though tetanus is rare in developed countries, the disease may be fatal, and preventive shots are given to anyone who might be exposed. For example, even though 15-year-old Brandon had a tetanus shot when he was a young child, the doctor gave him a tetanus booster when his cat bit him. Tetanus shots are both safe and inexpensive, and long-term immunization is recommended for everyone. If someone is exposed to tetanus and has not been protected recently, an injection with tetanus antitoxin—passive immunization—and a booster shot of toxoid—active immunization—are needed. Most infants in the United States are vaccinated against tetanus when they receive other injections, but doctors give booster shots of tetanus vaccine whenever there is any question about exposure to the bacteria. Tetanus shots are recommended for everyone every 10 years.

Do you know anyone who has had *pertussis,* or whooping cough? Gwen remembers terrible coughing spells that she had, mostly at night, when she was 8 years old. Every hour or so, she had a spell of more than a dozen coughs, one right after the other. During a coughing fit, she couldn't breathe. She gagged and choked and thought she might die. When the coughing stopped, she drew air into her lungs with the "whooping" sound that is characteristic of pertussis. The doctor explained that the pertussis bacteria were damaging her airways and producing a lot of sticky secretions. To get rid of the thick mucus, she had to cough and cough. Sometimes she even vomited after the violent coughing fits.

In the 1930s, almost 200,000 children in the United States caught whooping cough, and as many as 8,000 died each year.[5] The introduction and widespread use of pertussis vaccine in the United States has played an important role in greatly reducing these numbers. However, the disease still strikes about 6,000 children and infants annually.[6] Many of these children are not immunized according to the recommended schedule, and one-third are not immunized at all.

Many adults in the United States who are not ill carry the pertussis bacteria. These people are likely to infect the members of their household, especially infants who have not been vaccinated. In addition, some children who have a mild form of the disease spread it to others because it is not recognized as pertussis. Developing countries, where vaccines are not widely used, still have millions of cases of pertussis, leading to hundreds of thousands of deaths.[7]

Before 1991, on rare occasions, pertussis vaccine caused severe side effects, although probably no children died as a result. These problems, called adverse effects, are discussed in Chapter 6. Some parents refuse to let their children be vaccinated against pertussis due to possible side effects. But many children who were not vaccinated have died from the disease.

Late in 1991, a newer and safer pertussis vaccine became available. The old vaccine was made from whole, killed cells of the pertussis bacteria, but the new vaccine, called acellular vaccine, is made from only a few parts of the microbe. It is purer and safer, and the likelihood of fever and other reactions has fallen by half. Studies are continuing to find safer and more effective pertussis vaccines. The vaccine for diphtheria, tetanus, and pertussis (DTP) has been used for many years. However, the American Academy of Pediatrics recommends that the newer vaccine, called DTaP (which stands for diphtheria, tetanus, and acellular pertussis) be given to all children.

Chickenpox

Chickenpox, or *varicella zoster*, is a highly infectious viral disease. It begins with a skin rash consisting of itchy bumps that form small blisters and then become crusty scabs. The worst thing about it is usually the annoying and uncomfortable itchiness and the temptation to scratch.

In children, chickenpox is usually a mild disease, but in adults, it may be more serious. Adults who develop chickenpox are ten times more likely than children to require hospitalization or develop complications. Adults are twenty to thirty times more likely to die of chickenpox than children are.[8]

Each year, chickenpox accounts for about 15,000 hospitalizations, and about 100 children and adults in the United States die of the disease. Complications include pneumonia, severe bacterial infections of the skin caused by group A streptococci ("flesh-eating" bacteria), and brain infections that damage the nervous system permanently.[9]

Once you have had chickenpox, your body is immune to the disease. Mark's grandmother had chickenpox when she was a girl, so she was surprised to find out that the painful, scabby rash that she recently developed on her chest was caused by the same virus. The chickenpox virus remains hidden in your nervous system. It occasionally becomes reactivated, generally in people

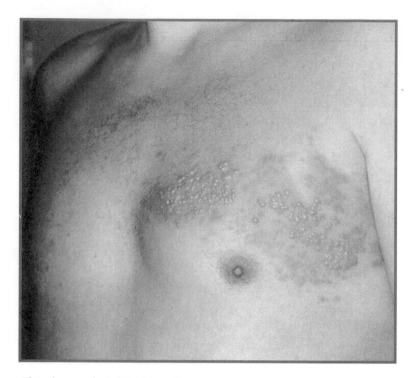

Shingles may look like this rash.

over the age of 50, and causes a painful rash known as *shingles* or *herpes zoster.*

Doctors are urging parents to have their children vaccinated against chickenpox with the vaccine that became available in 1995. Scientists tested the vaccine for 10 years in the United States and for 20 years in Japan. All tests found that the vaccine was safe and provided long-term protection.[10] By 1999, nine states required vaccination against chickenpox before children enter school.[11] One shot of vaccine for chickenpox produces immunity in 95 percent of children under 13, but two doses are recommended for older teens and adults.

The chickenpox vaccine is so new that many teenagers and adults did not receive it routinely along with other shots. If you do not know whether you had chickenpox or have been vaccinated against the disease, you can have a blood test that tells whether you have developed any signs of immunity.

Measles, Mumps, and Rubella (MMR) Vaccine

You were probably vaccinated against measles, mumps, and rubella at the same time. Two doses of this vaccine, often called MMR—the first at 12 to 15 months of age and the second at 4 to 6 years of age—provide lifetime immunity to all three diseases in 99 percent of those vaccinated. A single dose of MMR gives immunity about 95 percent of the time.[12] Although measles is no longer common in the United States, it kills many infants in developing countries.

Quarantine signs for measles once were common.

Measles is a severe viral illness that is easily spread. Although it is usually considered a childhood disease, people can catch it at any age. At an army base, Lieutenant Hyde ate his meals with other officers and their families. When 5-year-old Teddy first had measles, he ate with the 25-year-old lieutenant, who was unaware of how easily the disease was spread. Within the next few weeks, Hyde had the measles. Then a dozen soldiers in his camp became infected, and they spread measles to others. At first, many of the men thought having a childhood disease was funny, but when they developed fever, red eyes, and a cough, followed by a red blotchy rash, they were not amused. Later, they learned that measles can have serious complications, such as pneumonia and encephalitis, or infection of the brain.

Before the measles vaccine was approved in 1963, more than 500,000 cases of measles occurred in the United States each year, with about 400 to 500 deaths. After the vaccine was available, the number of cases dropped to less than 2,000 over a period of two decades.

A failure to vaccinate children at the proper age caused a recurrence of measles between 1989 and 1991. In 1998, the CDC announced that the United States had the lowest confirmed number of cases of measles since 1912, when doctors were required to report it. However, no vaccine is 100 percent perfect. In Alaska, a 1998 increase in measles resulted in the revaccination of many children and an order that schoolchildren have documentation of two doses of the measles vaccine.[13]

Mumps is a contagious viral disease described 2,500 years ago by the Greek physician Hippocrates. In most instances, mumps affects people between the ages of 5 and 15 years. It generally begins with symptoms like those of a slight, feverish cold. Painful swelling of the salivary glands in front of the ears and under the jaw soon follows. Although the swelling may be just on one side, it usually occurs on both sides. The swelling makes it difficult to chew and swallow. Mumps usually lasts about 1 week.

About half the cases of mumps are characterized by a mild inflammation of the lining of the spinal cord. Sometimes boys

Sometimes mumps used to spread through all the children in a family before a vaccine against the disease became available.

beyond the age of puberty experience pain and swelling of the testicles. Less frequently, girls may suffer from involvement of the ovaries. Adult men may become sterile as a result of infection with the mumps. Women who are infected during their first trimester of pregnancy may miscarry.[14]

Experts consider the mumps vaccine, which is made from weakened, attenuated virus, to be quite safe. It rarely has any side effects. Because mumps is still present in the United States, decreased use of the vaccine might lead to an upswing in the number of cases such as the one that occurred between 1989 and 1991.

Rubella, or German measles, is a mild viral disease that causes a 3-day rash, swelling of the lymph glands, and feelings of tiredness. The rash may resemble that of a mild case of measles. Sometimes no rash occurs, and the illness is so mild that people are not even aware that they have it.

In most cases, rubella is not serious, but it can have a terrible effect on an unborn child when a woman is infected with rubella during the first few months of pregnancy. At birth, the infant may be mentally retarded, blind, or deaf. Or the child may be born with a heart defect. Between 1964 and 1965, about 12 million cases of rubella accounted for birth defects in about 20,000 children. Today, thanks to vaccinations, only about 200 cases of rubella and two to three cases of birth defects are reported each year.[15]

Haemophilus influenzae *Type b (Hib)*

Haemophilus influenzae type b (Hib) is a bacterium that can cause *meningitis*—inflammation of the lining of the spinal cord—with lasting brain damage. Infection is widespread. The bacterium usually infects children under the age of two. Although antibiotics can be used to treat Hib, it kills 1 out of every 20 children who suffer from the meningitis, and 1 in 5 is left mentally retarded, blind, deaf, or learning disabled.[16]

In 1990, a vaccine to prevent Hib was approved for children under 5 years of age, resulting in what some people have called a medical miracle.[17] Since 1988, cases of Hib in children in the United States have decreased 99 percent! Remember that it took many years of hard work to conquer smallpox, and in comparison, this period is relatively short. Experts consider the Hib vaccine to be completely safe. A few children experience soreness at the place where the shot was given, and about 2 percent develop a low-grade fever.

Influenza

In the fall of each year, you hear many people talk about influenza, or flu, and when they plan to get their "flu shot." Although these shots are recommended mainly for people who have medical problems such as asthma, kidney, and lung and heart disease, or are over the age of 65, young people are encouraged to protect themselves from the misery of the flu. Children can carry the flu virus, so some health experts suggest that they be immunized against it too.

Seventeen-year-old Brandon laughed at his friend Samantha because she decided to have a flu shot. He wasn't so amused several months later when he suddenly developed a fever, muscle pain, and a sore throat. In addition, a headache and dry cough made his life miserable for about 5 days. Brandon did not feel really well for several weeks. After that illness, Brandon decided to have a flu shot every year.

In 1918, many healthy young adults died in the widespread epidemic of Spanish flu. About 20 million people worldwide died of the flu that year, when the virus was especially virulent. Some experts predict the appearance of another killer virus, but vaccines that protect against all forms of the virus will probably prevent another serious epidemic. Every spring, experienced doctors get together to develop new vaccines to fight the kinds of virus that they expect to be most common during the next flu

An epidemic of influenza occurred just after World War I. This police-man wore a mask to protect himself from the flu.

season, which begins in the fall. Although a flu shot may not necessarily protect against the disease, it is 70 to 90 percent effective against the illness.

You may wish to consider adding influenza vaccine to your list of vaccinations, unless you are allergic to eggs or have a history of Guillain-Barré syndrome (GBS)—a disease of the nervous system that causes weakness and loss of feeling. In some years, the risk of developing GBS after a flu shot is 1.7 times higher than expected, which means that slightly more than one additional case of GBS per million persons occurs in people vaccinated against influenza. According to the Chief of Vaccine Safety and

Development at the National Immunization Program of the CDC, this finding has not led to changes in official recommendations concerning the flu vaccine. The chance of developing influenza, which causes more than 20,000 deaths each year in the United States, far outweighs the extremely small risk of developing GBS following influenza vaccination.[18]

Meningitis

Melanie was a healthy 18-year-old college freshman. She woke up one morning thinking she had the flu, and she felt worse as the day went on. By the time she went to the hospital the evening of the next day, she was in bad shape. Her kidneys failed, and she developed gangrene (destruction of the tissues) in her arms and legs. Melanie had meningococcal meningitis, which is caused by a type of bacteria known as meningococcus. She soon needed a kidney transplant, and all her limbs eventually had to be amputated.

A relatively small number of people get meningococcal meningitis each year—about 3,000. This disease is scary, because it initially appears to be a mild case of flu. Even with treatment, it can kill a healthy young person within hours. As many as 13 percent of affected people die, and of the survivors, 15 percent are left with permanent brain damage.[19]

The incidence of meningococcal meningitis seems to be increasing in young people between the ages of 15 and 24. College freshmen who live in dormitories are six times more likely to get the disease than college students in general, but researchers don't know why. They think that living in close quarters is a factor. If a person comes down with menigococcal meningitis, other people who live in the same household are 500 times more at risk of being infected than the rest of the population.[19]

In the fall of 1999, a federal advisory committee to the CDC recommended vaccination for all college freshmen who live in dormitories to protect them against meningitis. The number of cases of disease is relatively low, but vaccination could prevent the 15 to 20 deaths that occur among college students every year.

Until 1970, when a vaccination program was instituted, meningococcal meningitis was a serious problem among military recruits. Since then, the number of infections has been very low. Vaccination is not recommended for the general population because most people are not at risk.

What Vaccinations Do You Need?

If you do not know what vaccinations you have had, ask your doctor which ones you should have now. Some vaccines, such as the vaccine for chickenpox, may not have been given to you routinely because they are relatively new. Boosters to protect against tetanus are recommended every 10 years, but some injuries may require a tetanus shot at the time of the wound. If you are between the ages of 11 and 19, check your vaccination history to see if you need any of the vaccines listed in the following table.

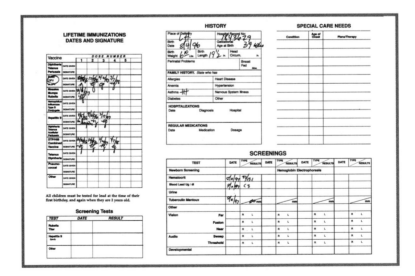

This lifetime health record, which gives a person's vaccination history, was issued by the New York City Department of Health. Try to get a your own vaccination history from your doctor, nurse, or local health office.

Recommended Immunizations for Older Children*

Vaccination	Notes
Measles, mumps, rubella (MMR)	Check with your doctor or nurse to make sure you have had your second dose.
Tetanus, diphtheria (Td)	If it has been more than 5 years since you received your last shot, you need a booster. Tetanus shots are needed every 10 years.
Varicella (chickenpox)	If you have not been previously vaccinated and have never had chickenpox, you should be vaccinated against this disease.
Hepatitis A	Talk to your doctor, nurse, or other health-care professional about health risks.
Hepatitis B	You need three doses of this vaccine if you have not already received them.
Influenza vaccine (flu shot)	Some experts recommend annual flu shots for everyone. Flu shots every fall are recommended for people with chronic diseases, such as heart disease, asthma, or diabetes.
Pneumococcal vaccine	Talk to your doctor, nurse, or other health-care professional about health risks.

*If you are between the ages of 11 and 19, check your vaccination history to see if you need any of the following vaccines.

Note: The complete recommended immunization schedule for children is published by the Centers for Disease Control and Prevention (CDC). To report an adverse vaccine reaction, ask your doctor, nurse, or health department to file a Vaccine Adverse Event Report form.

6

Does Immunization Cause Harm?

NATURALLY, ALL PARENTS are concerned about their children's health. But about 1 percent of parents in the United States refuse vaccinations for their children because they believe immunization is not safe or not necessary, despite the recommendations of the CDC and other scientific and medical organizations.[1] There are many sources of information about vaccinations, but not all of them are equally reliable. Dawn and Scott Richardson decided that they did not want their infant daughter Alexa to have the usual round of immunizations. They began to worry about vaccine safety when their cat went into shock after an immunization and the veterinarian had to revive him. Then they heard about a 3-month-old baby who died after receiving a series of immunizations, and this confirmed their doubts.

Concern about the safety of the pertussis vaccine in the early 1980s led to the formation of groups of concerned citizens such as the National Vaccine Information Center (NVIC; formerly known as Dissatisfied Parents Together). Publication of various articles and books has educated people about the possible risks of vaccination. Critics of vaccine programs are very emotional about the subject of possible vaccine-associated injuries. Many of them believe their children have been severely harmed by vaccinations. Only rarely have these children actually been hurt, however.

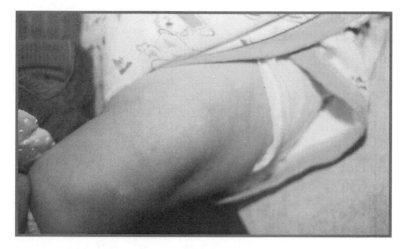

Some vaccinations leave red marks on the skin for a short time.

Other people object to vaccination for religious or ethical reasons, and still others believe it is not up to the government to tell them how to care for their children. Some parents put off taking their children for vaccinations to spare them pain or anxiety.

You probably know what it feels like to get a shot. Shots may cause a bit of pain and occasionally some immediate side effects, most of which are not serious. The most common are soreness, redness, and swelling at the site of injection, slight fever, and sometimes achy feelings throughout the body for about 24 hours. Very rarely do vaccinations cause severe allergic reactions. However, a small number of people are allergic to some of the substances used in the manufacture of vaccines.

Vaccine Additives

Some opponents of vaccination maintain that vaccines contain a "witch's brew" of toxic chemicals. They ask why deadly substances are added to medicines. A mercury compound known as thimerosal has been cited as an example.[2] Although mercury can be poisonous, the small amount of thimerosal that is added to vaccines contains very little mercury, and there is no evidence that it has caused harm. However, vaccine manufacturers are working to reduce or eliminate the use of thimerosal. In fact, some contact lens solutions and throat sprays contain thimerosal. Many chemical substances and medicines that benefit us can be dangerous or lethal when used improperly. Numerous foods and medicines contain chemicals to preserve them.

Chemicals are added to vaccines to preserve them and also to inactivate the viruses or bacteria. Some of the additives, which are known as adjuvants, help stimulate the production of antibodies. Substances that may be found in vaccines are egg protein, monosodium glutamate (MSG), and sulfites. Egg protein is present in vaccines that are prepared by using chicken eggs, and

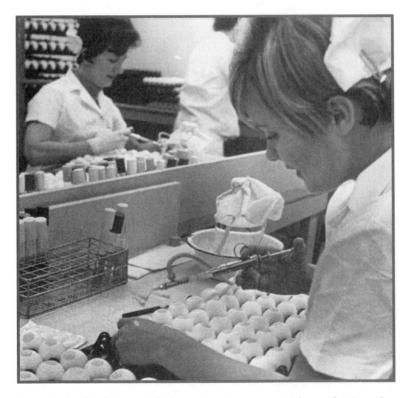

Inoculating fertile eggs with flu vaccine is one step in the production of flu vaccine.

MSG and sulfites are used as preservatives. You may be familiar with MSG as a flavor enhancer used in Asian foods. Sulfites are also found in foods, such as dried fruits, and in some wines and other alcoholic beverages.

If you know you are allergic to any substances, such as eggs or sulfites, for example, or if you have had a reaction to any vaccine in the past, be sure to tell your doctor, nurse, or other health-care professional. If you are concerned about the additives in vaccines or about possible side effects, you should ask for an explanation. The CDC has developed Vaccine Information Statements that must be given to patients and their parents or guardians. These information sheets give a clear explanation of the benefits and risks of each vaccine. The CDC and other government agencies publish many pamphlets and fact sheets that you can order, and the CDC maintains an Internet site. See the To Find Out More section at the back of this book.

Fears about Contaminated Vaccines

Some people believe vaccines contain infectious organisms that may cause disease. One widely publicized incident that occurred in 1955 concerned a batch of polio vaccine. Of all the people who received the vaccine, 60 developed polio. In addition, 89 other people who were in contact with them also developed the disease. Errors on the part of the manufacturer and lack of proper supervision by a government regulatory agency caused this disaster.[3] Two lots of inactivated polio vaccine contained some live polio virus.

This tragic mistake made many people ask if the risk of vaccination was greater than the risk of the disease. But recently, the Food and Drug Administration (FDA) has recalled vaccine lots that raised concerns before problems could develop.

Another concern is the possible contamination of a vaccine by an undetected virus. Between 1955 and 1963, millions of American children received the original inactivated polio vaccine. Researchers later found that some of the vaccine contained a monkey virus called SV40, which can cause cancer in monkeys. Although this virus can be transmitted to humans, it does not cause disease in people. The polio vaccine had been manufactured using monkey kidney cells, and the process used did not completely inactivate SV40. After 1961, improved control and testing methods were introduced. The vaccine was prepared using a species of monkeys that does not harbor SV40. Since then there has been no evidence of SV40 in polio vaccine.

Although some researchers have named SV40 as the cause of certain cancers in humans, studies show no increase in cancer rates among the people who received the contaminated vaccine after more than 30 years of careful follow-up. In addition, there is absolutely no evidence for the unfounded and mistaken belief that SV40 can trigger AIDS.[4]

Undiscovered infectious organisms are always a potential danger when human or animal tissues or blood are used, so researchers are constantly looking for newer and safer ways of making vaccines to eliminate the chance of contamination with infectious agents. The FDA requires that manufacturers follow strict procedures in the making of vaccines, and the vaccines are subject to many different tests to detect various infectious agents that might be present. The vaccines are also tested in animals before they are used in humans. Chapters 8 and 9 contain more information about the manufacture and testing of new vaccines.

Some antivaccine literature contains completely unsubstantiated reports suggesting that the American Cancer Institute and the WHO deliberately manufactured HIV, the virus that causes AIDS. Supposedly, this HIV was incorporated into a smallpox vaccine and given to people in central Africa.[5] False and frightening myths such as this one are misleading and confusing when reported along with legitimate scientific studies.

Some people believe that when someone is vaccinated, genetic material from the virus invades the person's cells and changes the genetic structure. This is not true. Some viruses, known as retroviruses, do invade the genetic matter of their host cells, how-

This teenage boy contracted AIDS from a blood transfusion. Some people wrongly believe that AIDS can come from vaccinations.

ever. HIV is one such virus. But there is no evidence of HIV or any other retrovirus in any vaccines.

Vaccines as Scapegoats

Some of the opponents of vaccination claim that it may cause a wide range of harmful conditions. These include learning disabilities, autism (a serious mental condition), seizures, impulsive violence, juvenile delinquency, cancer, diabetes (a chronic disease caused by a defect in the production of insulin, the body's sugar-regulating hormone), and sudden infant death syndrome—SIDS, or the sudden and unexpected death of an apparently healthy infant.

These claims sound very scary, but are they based on reliable research? There is no good evidence that vaccines are responsible for any of these conditions. Most of the evidence for a connection between vaccinations and disease is gathered from reports of illness or death that occurred around the time of vaccination. Just because two events happen at about the same time does not mean that one causes the other. For instance, suppose you dream that your best friend was injured in a bicycle accident. If she skidded and fell off her bicycle a week later, would you feel responsible for her broken leg?

Blaming vaccinations for SIDS is an example of this mistaken reasoning. SIDS is one of the leading causes of infant death in the United States. In a typical case, a mother may enter her baby's room one morning and find the infant dead in its crib. She has no idea why the baby, a previously healthy infant, died. Placing babies on their backs to sleep seems to help prevent SIDS, and in 1992, the American Academy of Pediatrics (AAP) recommended this for all healthy infants under a year old. Before 1992, from 5,000 to 6,000 SIDS deaths were reported every year. Between 1992 and 1996, when many people started to follow the AAP's advice, the number of deaths dropped to less than 4,000.[6]

As opponents of vaccination point out, most deaths from SIDS occur during the first year of life, which happens to be when infants receive DTP shots. Many of these deaths occur in children who have recently been vaccinated, but this does not mean that vaccination is the cause. Just by chance alone, a certain number of deaths could be expected to occur after immunization. The scientists at the U. S. Institute of Medicine reviewed many controlled studies comparing groups of immunized children with nonimmunized children. They reported that the number of SIDS deaths associated with DTP immunizations was about the number to be expected by chance. The studies found either no association with immunization or even a decreased risk of SIDS in immunized children.[7]

Newspaper reports have drawn attention to suggestions that the vaccine against hepatitis B might cause a disease of the nervous system known as multiple sclerosis (MS), but the National

Multiple Sclerosis Society and other groups claim there is no evidence of a link between the vaccine and MS. After some reports in France provoked fears that there might be a connection between hepatitis B vaccine and MS, the French National Drug Surveillance Committee studied the situation. They checked recipients of more than 60 million doses of hepatitis B vaccine and found that the frequency of diseases of the nervous system, including MS, that might be linked to the vaccination was lower than the frequency of MS in the general population.[8] Researchers found no confirmed scientific evidence that the vaccine against hepatitis B causes chronic fatigue disorder (a mysterious, exhausting disease), MS, rheumatoid arthritis, or other diseases of the immune system.[9]

Still, controversy about the safety of vaccination against hepatitis B continues. In January 1999, experts associated with The Vaccine Initiative, a special project of the Infectious Disease Society of America and the Pediatric Infectious Diseases Society, stated that figures released by the NVIC incorrectly presented information about the risks of side effects associated with hepatitis B vaccine. The NVIC claimed that there are more serious reactions from the vaccine than there are cases of the actual disease in children under the age of 14.

Opponents of vaccination quote widely varying statistics concerning the number of deaths connected with adverse reactions to vaccines. These statistics refer to the number of reports of deaths occurring after vaccinations, not deaths proved to have been caused by a vaccine. One source claims that as many as 943 children in the United States are killed every year by the DTP vaccine.[10] However, according to the CDC, which investigated and followed up all deaths reported between 1990 and 1992, only one death was associated with a vaccine.[11]

Investigators proved that many of these reported deaths were caused by totally unrelated conditions such as cancer, choking on a foreign body, and congenital heart disease.[12] The risk of death from any vaccine used at present is extremely low.

How Adverse Reactions Are Monitored

In response to these concerns about childhood vaccines, the U.S. Congress passed the National Childhood Vaccine Injury Act in 1986. This act established the National Vaccine Injury Compensation Program (VICP), which is a federal system designed to compensate individuals or families who have been injured by childhood vaccines. The vaccines are diphtheria, pertussis, measles, mumps, rubella, polio, Hib, hepatitis B, and chickenpox. Claims may be made for any injury or death thought to be the result of one of these vaccines. People can make claims for vaccine-caused injuries such as severe shock (anaphylactic shock), paralytic polio, and brain damage. A physician from the U.S. Department of Health and Human Services reviews claims, and then they are decided at hearings in a federal court.

The National Vaccine Injury Act also established the Vaccine Adverse Events Reporting System (VAERS), to which anyone can report a suspected reaction to any vaccine. Health-care professionals are required to notify VAERS, which is run by the FDA and CDC, of any adverse events after immunization for the childhood diseases covered by the VICP. A VAERS report does not mean that a vaccine caused an event, however, but only that it occurred.

The congressional act also specified that communication about the possible risks of vaccination improve. It required that pamphlets with information about these risks be given to people when they or their children are vaccinated.[13]

To study the risks of childhood vaccines, the Institute of Medicine established a Vaccine Safety Committee, composed of experts in such areas as infectious diseases, internal medicine, microbiology, and immunology. They reviewed all the available scientific and medical literature in English and other languages, including more than 7,000 abstracts of scientific studies and more than 2,000 books and articles! In addition, they used information from VAERS and other reporting systems, along with individual case reports from VAERS (which numbered 17,000 at the time of the review in 1992). The committee also held scientific workshops, where other experts made presentations. It held several public meetings so that people could present their opinions and comments.

The committee had a hard time making sense of all the information and drawing conclusions from it because there were many gaps and limitations in the data. Reasons for the difficulties included the following:

- It was not possible to find a large number of unvaccinated people to compare with vaccinated people, because about 90 percent of individuals have been vaccinated.
- Many of the studies about vaccine risks did not involve enough people or did not monitor people for a sufficiently long time.
- Reports of vaccine-associated risks may have been inaccurate or incomplete. Not all side effects may have been reported. Duplicate reports for the same patient were common and often hard to identify, and medical information on the forms was sometimes incomplete.

The committee called for more research, better surveillance, better follow-up of reports of serious adverse events and deaths, increased efforts to make sure that reporting was more complete, and the establishment of disease registries for rare conditions.[14]

The Vaccine Safety Committee also analyzed all the evidence regarding the possible association between vaccines and specific adverse effects such as brain damage, seizures, and other nervous system disorders, as well as SIDS and severe allergic reactions. Although it found that some vaccines caused a small number of serious reactions, it discovered no connections in other instances. For example, SIDS was not associated with vaccinations, nor did the improved Hib vaccine cause an increased risk of influenza immediately after vaccination. The risk for most of these serious adverse events ranged from one in several thousand to one in millions. The chance of a serious reaction to a vaccine is so rare that it is difficult to determine exactly.

Of course, no vaccine is completely without risk, and the serious illness or death of even one person after vaccination is a tragedy. But the risk of death or severe aftereffects of a disease are many times higher than the risks of immunization. The benefits of vaccination must always be balanced against the risks. Consider smallpox, which has been eradicated worldwide. The possible complications resulting from giving the smallpox vaccine now outweigh any possible risk of contracting the disease. Therefore, the vaccine is no longer recommended for the general population. It is recommended only for people who work in laboratories with the group of viruses that cause smallpox.

7

Questions About Vaccinations

MANY PEOPLE HAVE doubts about vaccination. Some of the most often asked questions are listed below, along with their answers.

QUESTION 1: *Are there natural herbs and foods that can act as an alternative to vaccination by strengthening a person's immune system?*

ANSWER 1: There are no proven substitutes for immunization, and many people with healthy immune systems become infected and die of diseases that could have been prevented by vaccination. For example, at least five previously healthy people died of chickenpox in 1997. As you have learned, a person's immune system must have produced antibodies against the virus to protect someone from chickenpox. This requires either exposure to the disease or vaccination. An unvaccinated child must fight the disease without the help of the antibodies that would have developed after vaccination.

QUESTION 2: *Infants sometimes get shots against many diseases at the same time. Is it possible that all those shots weaken and overload their immune systems?*

ANSWER 2: Infants develop in a germ-free environment inside the mother's uterus, and at birth they enter a world that is full of microorganisms. Every day brings constant exposure to many new bacteria and viruses. It is unlikely that adding a few new antigens in the form of immunizations would put much extra burden to an infant's immune system.[1] It is known that some natural viral infections can temporarily weaken the immune system, and some researchers have found that similar mild, short-lived effects occur after measles immunization. Because reduced resistance to infections is possible, scientists are always on the alert for any problems as new vaccines are being developed.[2] But numerous studies have found that vaccinations—even multiple vaccinations given at the same time—have no ill effects on a child with a normal immune system.[3]

A few individuals have conditions that make it dangerous for them to be vaccinated. People whose immune systems are defective—such as children or adults who have HIV—should not receive vaccines that contain live virus, because they might develop severe or fatal infections. They can receive other vaccines that do not contain live virus, however. Exposure to people who have received live oral polio virus vaccine can be dangerous for a child with HIV, because the people can excrete live virus from the vaccine and transmit it to a child who does not have a fully functional immune system.

QUESTION 3: *Sometimes people who get a disease have already been vaccinated against it. So why vaccinate against this disease?*

ANSWER 3: It is true that during an epidemic, some people who have been vaccinated against a disease may become victims of the illness. Of the people who get sick, those who have been vaccinated often outnumber those who have not been vaccinated. If vaccines really work, how could this happen? Vaccinated people may get sick for two reasons. First, no vaccine is 100 percent effective. According to the CDC, most vaccines for childhood diseases are 85 percent to 95 percent effective.[4] Second, the great majority of people in developed countries such as the United States have been vaccinated, so the total number of vaccinated people is very large, much larger than the number of unvaccinated people.

For example, suppose your school has 1,000 students, and no one there has ever had measles. Only five students have not been vaccinated against the disease. Everyone is then exposed to measles, and the result is that all five of the unprotected students become infected, while 9 of the 995 immunized students are also infected. This is not surprising, because we know that the vaccine fails to produce immunity in a small percentage of people.

In this example, measles infected almost twice as many vaccinated as unvaccinated students. But 100 percent of the unvaccinated students got measles, and less than 1 percent of the vaccinated students were infected. If no one had been immunized, it is likely that you and all your schoolmates would have caught measles.

QUESTION 4: *Weren't some diseases already starting to disappear before vaccines were widely used?*

ANSWER 4: This is true to some extent. There is no doubt that good nutrition, an improved standard of living, and better sanitation—for example, pure water supplies and refrigera-

Improved sanitation has led to medical progress. With sewage treatment, bacteria can be filtered out before water is discharged into a river. This worker is holding samples of treated and untreated sewage.

tion of perishable foods—have influenced the spread of disease. Advances in medical treatment such as the development of antibiotics have also reduced the number of deaths from some diseases that used to be life threatening. Before antibiotics, you risked dying from a bacterial skin infection if it spread throughout your body. Untreated pneumococcal pneumonia kills one of every four people who get it, but treatment with penicillin now cures most people. Infectious diseases seem to have a natural history of running in cycles, with up-and-down periods. Throughout history, there have been epidemics of the bubonic plague—the Black Death—which once killed an estimated 25 percent of the population of Europe. Then the disease subsided, only to flare up again.

Still, the myth that vaccines have not contributed to the decline of infectious diseases persists. For example, one author claims that deaths from measles declined significantly in the United States and England during the first half of the twentieth century, before the introduction of the measles vaccine in 1963.[5] But the sad fact is that before the vaccine, almost every child in the United States got measles, and hundreds of children died every year.[6]

Between 1989 and 1991, there was a sharp increase in the number of measles cases, and more than 120 people died. Immunization foes seized on this outbreak as proof that the vaccine was not effective. But that was not the reason. Many African-American and Hispanic children had not been vaccinated. As a result, they got sick, and this caused the increase.

Measles is one of nine diseases on a list prepared by the CDC that compares the number of cases in the prevaccine era to the number in 1996, when about 90 percent of the U.S. population received immunizations. In 1941, the number of reported cases of measles was nearly 900,000; in 1996, it was about 500 cases.[7] The other diseases on the CDC list all show similar dramatic reductions of more than 99 percent. Only about 10,000 cases of vaccine-preventable diseases occurred in 1996; millions of these diseases were reported before vaccines were used. This tremendous decline in the number of cases must certainly be linked to the widespread use of vaccines.

So if improved sanitation and nutrition are responsible for the disappearance of diseases such as measles, then we should expect a similar decline in the number of cases of chickenpox. But this is not happening. During most of the twentieth century, about 4 million cases of chickenpox occurred each year in the United States. Almost all young children got the disease, and the risk was probably as great for them as it was when their grandmothers were children. No vaccine was available until 1995.[8] If widespread use of the vaccine results in a drop in the number of cases of chickenpox—as predicted—then this would be further proof that vaccines prevent disease.

QUESTION 5: *Most diseases for which children are vaccinated are very rare in the United States now, so why should we vaccinate anyone against them?*

ANSWER 5: Although most vaccine-preventable diseases are now rare in the United States, this is not true in other parts of the world. Remember that we are just a plane ride away from any disease outbreak. If we did not have the protection given by vaccinations, someone could easily bring a disease into the United States and cause an epidemic here. For example, measles is common in many other countries. In 1996, 47 cases of measles in the United States were imported from other countries.[9]

Studies performed in several countries have shown that the disease rate has increased following a decrease in immunizations. During the 1970s, concern about the safety of the pertussis vaccine used at that time led to a rapid decline in pertussis immunizations in the United Kingdom. Within the next several years, epidemics occurred. There were more than 100,000 cases and 36 deaths from pertussis there between 1971 and 1979.[10]

If immunizations were discontinued, widespread epidemics would occur again in the United States, as they have in the past, because the viruses and bacteria that cause vaccine-preventable diseases still exist in many places. One person with a highly contagious disease can infect numbers of unprotected people who have no antibodies because they have not been vaccinated or exposed to the disease. Even though these diseases are rare in the United States, it is important that everyone be immunized against them. For example, several years ago a young boy died of diphtheria in this country. He was the only child in his class who had not been vaccinated against the disease.[11]

QUESTION 6: *Aren't childhood illnesses mild and therefore less dangerous than the possible risks of vaccination?*

ANSWER 6: Not really. The risk of death or injury from vaccines is very low, as discussed in Chapter 6, but vaccine-preventable diseases cause high rates of death and disability. For example, diphtheria kills 1 of every 20 people who get the disease. Tetanus is a dangerous killer of newborn babies of unimmunized mothers in underdeveloped countries. Pertussis kills 1 of 200 infants who get whooping cough. No one has proved that the DTP vaccine causes death.[12]

Contrary to popular belief, chickenpox is a serious illness. Of the 4 million people in the United States who get this disease each year, 100 die. Adults are more than 20 times more likely to die than children.[13] Childhood diseases are not just a nuisance. They are not always mild and self-limiting, and the risk of death or serious consequences is real. Protection from disease by immunization far outweighs the slight risk from vaccination.[14]

QUESTION 7: *Is it true that the polio vaccine caused an increase in polio cases after years of decline?*

ANSWER 7: Yes, the only children in the United States who have had polio are those who received the oral live virus. Before the polio vaccine was available, between 13,000 and 20,000 cases of paralytic polio reportedly occurred in the United States every year. Now, "wild" polio here has been wiped out.[15] In 1999, not one case of the disease was reported. Infection after vaccination is extremely rare, but to reduce the risk still more, the CDC has recommended that doctors give the inactivated form instead of the live oral form of vaccine.

Do you have any more concerns? You can find answers to some of your questions by asking a doctor, nurse, or other health-care professional or by consulting the To Find Out More section at the back of this book.

8

New Ways to Make and Give Vaccines

MANY PEOPLE AVOID immunization for themselves or their children because they are afraid of needles. Getting a vaccination has always meant having an injection, but in addition to the painful jab, there are other problems with this method. Vaccines need proper storage, and needles and syringes are expensive. In some developing countries, refrigeration is often unavailable, and needles are sometimes reused without proper sterilization, resulting in spread of disease. The WHO has emphasized the urgency of developing safer ways of delivering vaccines.

Scientists at the WHO are also working to reduce the number of vaccine doses needed for long-lasting protection against disease. Tetanus is one disease for which you need more than one shot. After the initial injection with tetanus toxoid, individuals need a booster shot every 10 years. Remember the African boy Yusif, who died of tetanus? (See Chapter 5.) If vaccination against a disease such as tetanus could be completed in one or two doses, and there were no need for booster shots, it would be a lot more convenient. More people would receive vaccinations, which would mean fewer of them would die.

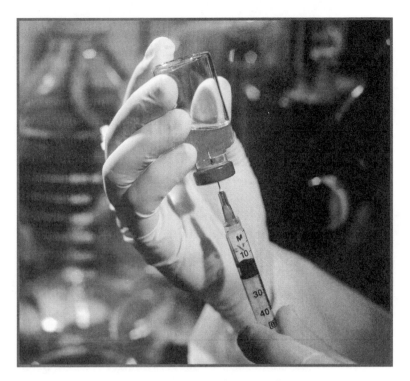

Disease can spread if vaccines are not administered properly.

New Ways of Giving Vaccines: Avoiding the Needle

Scientists are working on more than a dozen vaccines that can provide protection without needle sticks. Nasal sprays, skin patches, and time-release pellets are some new ways of delivering vaccines. Skin patches allow the vaccine to be absorbed slowly through the skin. Tiny pellets or "microspheres" that release vaccine over a long period of time can be taken by mouth or inhaled in the form of a nasal spray.

Most infections such as colds, flu, diarrhea, and sexually transmitted diseases (such as gonorrhea) enter the body through the mucous membranes. The mucous membranes are the tissues that line the body cavities—the mouth, nose, breathing passages, digestive tract, and the urinary and genital tracts. The mucous membranes act as gatekeepers, heading off harmful microbes before they reach organs inside the body. Vaccines applied to these tissues trigger the immune system more effectively.

Vaccines in the form of nasal sprays may be available in the near future. You may soon get a flu vaccination by inhaling a nasal spray instead of having a shot. Traditional flu vaccine uses killed, inactivated virus to produce an immune reaction. A new spray vaccine contains live, weakened virus that stimulates an immune response in the nose and throat. However, the virus cannot invade the lungs or other parts of the body because it is unable to survive in temperatures that are warmer than those in the area around the nose and throat.[1] Vaccines in the form of nasal sprays that act against several diseases, including a type of bacterial pneumonia and a severe diarrhea, as well as HIV are in the works.

Oral vaccines are not really new. As you have learned, Sabin developed an oral polio vaccine more than 40 years ago. You may have eaten a sugar cube soaked with vaccine to protect you against polio. (See Chapter 3 for a discussion of polio.)

Now an oral vaccine is used to fight typhoid, a serious disease that causes diarrhea, abdominal pain, and fever. An injectable vaccine against typhoid has long been available. Scientists are developing and testing numerous oral vaccines, including one that protects against the bacterium *Helicobacter pylori,* the microorganism that causes stomach ulcers, as well as some that work against diarrhea.

Researchers once thought a vaccine had solved the rotavirus problem. Rotavirus, the most common cause of severe diarrhea in infants and young children in the United States, is a serious problem around the world. Viruses in the rotavirus group cause this very contagious illness, which is easily spread from one child to another by contaminated hands or objects. Infection leads to diarrhea and vomiting. In infants, the resulting loss of water from

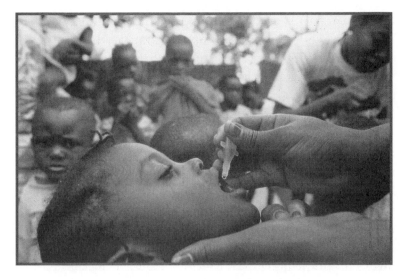

This child, who lives in the Congo, receives the oral polio vaccine.

the body and dehydration is especially life threatening. Almost all children get rotavirus during their first 3 to 5 years of life. Every year the disease may kill as many as 100 children in the United States and nearly 1 million children in developing countries.

One problem with oral vaccines is finding a way to keep them from being destroyed by the acid and other chemicals in the digestive tract. With the rotavirus vaccine, researchers prevented this by mixing the vaccine with a special protective solution and by having children drink milk half an hour before taking the vaccine. The milk helped counteract the acid normally present in the stomach. After children swallowed the live rotavirus vaccine, the virus reproduced in the stomach and stimulated production of protective antibodies. It did not cause illness, and the only side effect was mild fever. The vaccine reduced the incidence of severe diarrhea by up to 90 percent, and the rotavirus vaccine was approved by the FDA in September 1998.[2]

This seemed to be a success story—an easy-to-take vaccine that could save lives, reduce illness and hospital stays, and save more than $1 billion dollars a year in the United States. But less than a year later, a problem developed. In the summer of 1999, after about 1.5 million doses of the vaccine had been given, the Vaccine Adverse Event Reporting System (VAERS) received reports of at least 15 cases of intussusception—a type of bowel blockage. Although there was no proof of a definite connection between the vaccine and the bowel obstruction, the CDC recommended that use of the vaccine be put on hold until scientists could study the problem further.[3]

Imagine eating a banana to prevent hepatitis or drinking goat's milk to protect against disease. Some day, plants and animals could become a reliable and safe source of vaccines. Scientists already know how to introduce foreign genetic material into plants to make them resistant to agricultural pests. Now some researchers are using the same methods to inject harmless pieces of microbes into plants. The plants incorporate these particles into the genetic material of their cells, and when the plant cells reproduce, they also make copies of the microbe.

Using potatoes, researchers have attempted to develop an oral vaccine to fight another type of severe diarrhea. A strain of *Escherichia coli* bacteria causes this illness, which affects children around the world. Researchers grew potatoes that contained harmless proteins from the bacteria. When they fed the potatoes to mice, the mice developed antibodies to the bacteria. Human volunteers who ate the potatoes also developed antibodies. Scientists plan to experiment with other foods such as bananas and tomatoes.

You may not be able to eat your vaccines in your vegetables just yet, but scientists are working hard to make it possible. Before this kind of oral vaccine—that is, a vaccine already incorporated into your food—can be put to use, there are still many problems to be solved. For example, no one knows how much of these foods a person would have to eat or drink for protection.

Animals, too, may someday be converted into vaccine factories. Researchers have already been able to induce mice to manufacture a protein from the parasite that causes malaria. They have also bred goats whose milk contains the same malaria antigen. Drinking the milk might protect people against malaria, but so far, no human studies have taken place.[4]

Tooth decay might become history if a scientist in London is successful in perfecting a vaccine against the microbe that causes it. *Streptococcus mutans* is a bacterium that lives in everyone's mouth. It feeds on sugars that stick to your teeth, producing acids that eat away the tooth enamel and cause cavities. Scientist Julian Ma made a vaccine containing antibodies to the microbe and applied the vaccine to the teeth of volunteers. The antibodies in the vaccine prevented the bacteria from sticking to their teeth, and their mouths remained free of the bacteria for several months.[5] This vaccine is topical—it is applied to an area of the body, like a skin patch.

New Ways of Making Vaccines

For 200 years, since Dr. Jenner's time, vaccines have usually been made with microbes that were either alive but weakened, or killed. But researchers have discovered that vaccines do not have to be made from a whole microbe. Just one or more small parts of a microbe can provoke an immune response. Often there are fewer side effects if a vaccine is made from these small parts of the microbe, rather than the entire organism.

Sometimes a *subunit vaccine,* a vaccine that uses one or more parts of the disease-causing organism, is made by taking the microbe apart. But there is another method—*recombinant genetic engineering,* which is also called recombinant DNA technology. Researchers insert bits of *DNA,* the genetic material, from the cells of one organism into another. The second organism acts as a host. DNA carries instructions about certain jobs, such as making proteins. After the bits of DNA are inserted into the host organism, the cells of the host follow the directions contained in the inserted DNA. In this way, bacteria, yeasts, and plant or animal cells can be made into vaccine factories, churning out copies of the subunits—the DNA bits. The researchers you read about earlier made edible vaccines in this way.

Sometimes harmless genetic material from one disease-causing organism is inserted into a weakened virus or bacterium. One especially large virus, the vaccinia virus, is used to make some vaccines in this way because it has lots of room for added genetic fragments. A vaccinia virus with several HIV genes is being tested as a vaccine to protect against HIV, the virus that causes AIDS. At present, this vaccine is not approved for general use in the United States.[6]

You may be one of the 83 percent of the children in the United States who have had an ear infection by the time they are 3 years old.[7] A bacterium called *Streptococcus pneumoniae* is the leading cause of ear infections in young children and also a cause of pneumonia and meningitis. A vaccine has been available since 1983, but the problem is that the current vaccine does not give protection to children who are younger than 2 years old or to some elderly people.

These streptococcal bacteria have special outer coats made of sugar molecules that disguise their antigens. The immature immune systems of younger children do not recognize them as harmful, and so they do not make antibodies to the bacteria. Now, researchers have hitched the sugar molecules of the outer coat to substances that the immune system can recognize more easily. These new vaccines, called *conjugate vaccines,* are better at stimulating the immune systems of children and the elderly to make antibodies against *S. pneumoniae.*[8]

A conjugate vaccine against Hib disease has been used since 1987. As you have learned, Hib was once a common cause of bacterial meningitis among infants and children in the United States. It killed 600 children every year, and left many others with serious aftereffects such as deafness, seizures, and mental retardation. Since use of the vaccine began, the incidence of Hib has declined by 97 to 99 percent, and fewer than 10 people died of the disease in 1995.[9]

Some scientists think they may someday immunize cocaine addicts against the drug by using conjugate vaccines. They have attached proteins to cocaine molecules to make a conjugate vaccine that should stimulate the immune system to produce antibodies. The antibodies would bind with cocaine in the body and prevent it from entering the brain.[10]

Genetic immunization is a new kind of vaccination that involves injecting pure genetic material, called "naked" DNA, from a disease-causing organism directly into a person's body. A *naked DNA vaccine* contains the genes that can trigger a person's immune system, but they cannot cause disease because certain genetic material necessary to the microbe has been omitted.[11] After a person gets an injection of this DNA vaccine, it goes into his or her body cells. The cells then produce proteins as directed by the DNA from the microbe. These proteins, which are subunits of the microbe, act as antigens and stimulate the person's immune system to make antibodies.

Experiments have demonstrated that naked DNA vaccines can protect mice from infection with the bacteria that cause tuberculosis and Lyme disease.[12] Researchers have found that a

Deer ticks carry the bacteria that cause Lyme disease. The new vaccine against Lyme disease can protect against the disease and prevent much suffering.

DNA vaccine against rabies was successful in monkeys, and it may be safer than some vaccines now in use. Traditional vaccines that are made from the brain tissues of animals can cause serious side effects in some people. Unlike conventional vaccines, the new DNA vaccines are simple to develop, effective, and able to survive high temperatures.

Tests of DNA vaccines in humans began in 1995, when people already infected with HIV received vaccines made with HIV genes. Since then, researchers have been testing other DNA vaccines in healthy humans, mainly to check for safety. Scientists worry that the injected DNA might cause a person's immune system to attack the body's own genetic material, but so far, the vaccines seem to be safe for humans.[13]

9

New Vaccines for Existing Diseases

MILLIONS OF PEOPLE around the world are affected by serious diseases that are difficult to prevent or cure—some old and some new. For example, AIDS has no cure. After the discovery of the first antibiotics, scientists hoped that "wonder drugs" could wipe out the infectious diseases that had always plagued humans. But microbes that cause disease will probably be with us forever. They multiply rapidly, and they *mutate,* or change, easily. When they mutate, they may produce drug-resistant forms, which can reproduce and quickly outnumber those that the drug kills. The drugs are then no longer effective. Although new drugs are constantly being developed, new vaccines are very important to prevent infection with some diseases, especially those that are difficult or impossible to treat with drugs or other methods. Scientists are working to discover vaccines to protect people from HIV and AIDS, tuberculosis, malaria, and cancer.

HIV

AIDS may be the most frightening disease of the twentieth century. HIV, the causal virus, attacks the immune system and gradually destroys it, leaving the affected person defenseless against a variety of other infections, one of which is eventually fatal. As almost everyone knows, the search for a vaccine to protect against AIDS is a high priority in the world of medicine. At the time this book is being written, almost two decades after AIDS first appeared, there is still no magic cure or vaccine to prevent the disease. Medicines that seem to hold it in check are available, and they allow affected people to live longer. However, these drugs are very expensive, they do not work for everyone, and they are not a cure. Like other microbes, HIV can mutate and produce forms that are resistant to these medicines.

HIV infects more than 30 million people worldwide, 90 percent of them in Africa and Asia. In some countries, the rate of infection more than doubled between 1994 and 1998. According to the CDC, at the end of 1997, approximately 372,000 people in the United States were living with HIV or AIDS.

How do you get HIV? The virus is spread by the exchange of blood or body fluids. You cannot get HIV from casual contact. Sexual contact is one means of spreading the virus, and the use of needles contaminated with HIV is another. The only way to prevent it is by avoiding risky behavior.

Scientists who are trying to develop effective vaccines against HIV disease face some very tough challenges. In other viral diseases such as polio, for which successful vaccines have been made, some people who develop the disease recover. But no one has ever recovered from HIV disease, because the immune system cannot fight HIV in the same way it fights other viral diseases. So researchers do not know what kind of antibodies might exist in the immune system of a person who recovers. They do not even know whether someone's immune system can protect itself by natural means.

What makes HIV especially hard to combat?

First, its main target is the immune system itself. It invades the key cells of the immune system, the lymphocytes known as helper T cells, which direct the various complicated immune responses. The virus "hijacks" the host's cellular machinery, reprogramming it to make more virus particles. In the process, it destroys the ability of host cells to function. HIV can remain

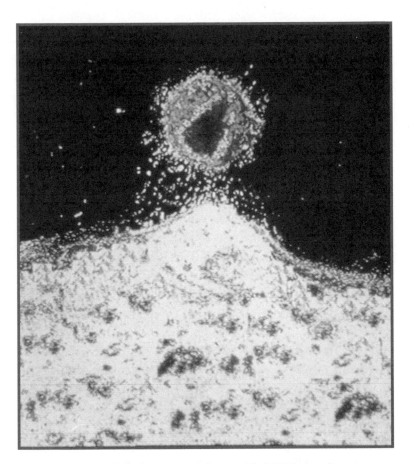

This photomicrograph shows a greatly magnified HIV virus bursting from the membrane of an infected lymphocyte (a white blood cell).

hidden in the T cells for a long time. Other parts of the body may also act as holding tanks for HIV, hiding the virus so that the immune system cannot detect it.

Second, unlike some other viruses, HIV can exist in the body outside of cells as free virus as well as inside infected cells. So, to be effective against HIV, a vaccine would need to stimulate the two main types of immunity—humoral immunity and cellular immunity.[1] Humoral immunity is the protection provided by antibodies in the defense against the free virus. Cellular immunity is the attacking of infected cells by the killer T lymphocytes of the immune system.

Scientists are trying to determine the best way to make a vaccine against HIV. As described in Chapter 2, traditional vaccines often use whole, weakened virus, but it would be very risky to use the whole virus in the case of HIV because of the danger of infection. For this reason, various subunits of the virus that cannot cause infection are used in the many experimental vaccines against HIV. In most of the tests, researchers have used vaccines made from proteins on the outer coat of the virus. They have used human volunteers in these tests. Unfortunately, although the vaccine stimulates production of antibodies on the part of the immune system, the antibodies don't work against HIV taken from infected patients.

Studies of several other strategies are underway. Some researchers have used protein fragments from inside HIV to make vaccines. Others have produced and tested several DNA vaccines made with naked DNA from HIV in both animals and humans. In some studies, scientists found that the vaccine protected the animals against HIV infection. Researchers are also experimenting with artificial copies of viral particles called pseudovirions.

Another experimental approach involves the insertion of some HIV genes into a weakened form of canarypox virus—a bird virus that is not harmful to people. The canarypox virus delivers the HIV genes to the body cells, where they produce HIV proteins. The proteins gain the attention of the body's immune system, causing it to make antibodies and killer T cells. Several of these vaccines are being tested in human volunteers.

Some researchers believe that using vaccines containing live weakened HIV would provide the best protection, but these vaccines have sparked the most controversy. Some scientists want to make a vaccine that protects people from HIV infection and does not cause AIDS. A group of physicians have volunteered to be the first human guinea pigs for this kind of experiment. But most researchers believe that more animal studies are needed before a live HIV vaccine is tested in humans.[2]

Chimpanzees can be infected with HIV, but only one chimpanzee is known to have developed full-blown AIDS. Full-blown disease develops in humans with HIV infection when the immune system can no longer fight back. Other infections invade the body and overwhelm the damaged immune system.

However, no one uses chimps for AIDS-related studies because they are an endangered species. Researchers sometimes use macaque monkeys because they can be infected with simian immunodeficiency virus (SIV), a virus that is similar to HIV and causes a disease that resembles AIDS. In fact, some scientists believe that SIV mutated and became HIV. Experiments have shown that live, weakened SIV vaccine has protected some monkeys from infection by naturally occurring SIV. But after observing the vaccinated monkeys for a long time, the researchers discovered that the vaccine itself infected some monkeys. They worry that the same thing might happen if humans are vaccinated with a similar HIV vaccine.

Another finding has forced scientists to conclude that a live AIDS vaccine, even a weakened form that is missing one or more genes, might be too dangerous to give to humans. A group of people infected for more than 10 years with such a weakened form of HIV had been healthy for many years, and their immune systems seemed able to resist the progression of HIV disease. However, they eventually started to show signs of AIDS. Even if no vaccine can protect against AIDS completely, investigators hope that they can make a partially effective vaccine that would help a person's own immune system keep HIV in check so that he or she could remain healthy and never develop AIDS.[3]

Tuberculosis

Tuberculosis, or TB, is a chronic bacterial infection that is spread through the air and infects the lungs. In some cases, it spreads to other organs. TB causes more deaths throughout the world today than any other infectious disease. One-third of the world's population is infected with the causal bacterium, although most of them never develop active TB. However, in people with weakened immune systems, especially those who have HIV, the TB microbes are likely to gain a stronghold and multiply, causing active disease.

When people with active TB cough or sneeze, they spread the bacteria in their lungs through the air, where other people can inhale them. Most people who happen to breathe in TB-causing microbes don't get the disease. Infection usually occurs only after prolonged exposure to someone with active TB. When inhaled bacteria reach the lungs, the immune system goes on alert and attacks the bacteria. Scavenger cells swallow the microbes. Other white blood cells release chemical signals, and the scavengers are walled off in tiny capsules called tubercles. In people with healthy immune systems, the infection is held in check, and the TB bacteria usually die. But if the person's resistance is low, the bacteria may escape from the tubercles. Infection may spread through the lungs, destroying lung tissue, and sometimes spreads to other organs. A positive skin test (PPD or Mantoux test) means that the person may have been infected with TB, but it does not necessarily mean that he or she has active TB. Most people who have been exposed to TB have positive tests.

Many Americans think that TB is a disease of the past. In the nineteenth century, TB killed more people in the United States than any other disease. By the middle of the twentieth century, better nutrition, sanitation, and medical care, along with the introduction of effective antibiotics, greatly reduced the number of cases. But in 1985, the number of cases began to rise again. More than 20,000 people in the United States have active TB, and an estimated 15 million more have latent, or inactive, infection. So TB is making another appearance.

Reasons for the increase in the number of cases include the following:

- Large numbers of people with HIV are susceptible to infections of TB and other diseases due to their weakened immune systems.
- Many immigrants from countries with high rates of TB and poor medical care have arrived in the United States.
- Although TB is curable if diagnosed and treated properly, many people receiving treatment for TB stop taking their medicine when they start feeling better. They do not realize that treatment must be continued for as long as 6 to 12 months to kill all the TB germs. Inadequate treatment may cause the bacteria to become resistant to the drugs.

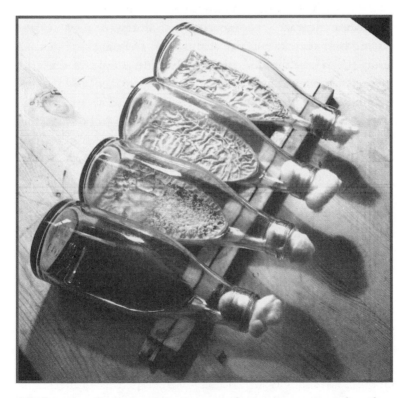

The bacterium Streptomyces griseus *produces streptomycin, a drug that is used to treat tuberculosis.*

The increase in the number of people who have MDR-TB— TB that is multidrug-resistant, or resistant to several drugs—is alarming. Half of the people with MDR-TB die even with treatment. If a person has both MDR-TB and HIV, the chance of death is 80 percent.

With the increase in MDR-TB, it is more important than ever that we find new drugs to treat it and a vaccine to prevent it. A vaccine known as BCG, which stands for bacille Calmette-Guérin, is made of live weakened bacteria. BCG is given to infants in parts of the world where TB is common, but it is not used in the United States. In adults, its usefulness varies from person to person. Although BCG prevents the spread of TB in the body, it does not prevent the initial infection.[4]

Researchers are experimenting with dozens of new vaccines to find ones that are effective against TB. These include vaccines using subunits of the TB bacterium, vaccines using live weakened strains of the bacterium, and vaccines with naked DNA. Some vaccines in the form of a spray are being tested. Before human testing begins, the vaccines are tested on mice, guinea pigs, rabbits, and monkeys.[5]

Malaria

You may wonder why anyone in the United States should be worried about a tropical disease such as malaria. But malaria is spreading rapidly, and it is no longer a rare or exotic illness in North America. Malaria is the deadliest of all tropical parasitic diseases, and one-third of the world's population lives in areas where it is common. Africa is one of these places.

According to WHO estimates, between 300 million and 500 million new cases of malaria occur each year, and 2 to 3 million people die of the disease. Ninety percent of all the malaria cases in the world occur in Africa, along with 90 percent of the deaths. Most of the dead are children under 5 years old. In the United States, the CDC receives reports of about 1,200 cases of malaria, but there are probably many more infected people who are not diagnosed. Most people become infected with malaria in other countries, but some people have been infected in the United States.

The microbes that cause malaria are carried by *Anopheles* mosquitoes, which transmit the disease to humans when they bite. The actual disease-causing organisms are parasites—organisms that depend on other living things and generally hurt their hosts. Four different types of the parasite infect humans, but the one known as *Plasmodium falciparum* is the most virulent. Falciparum malaria is responsible for almost all the deaths due to malaria in Africa. The other types of malaria are troublesome, but they are generally not deadly.

When a female *Anopheles* mosquito bites someone to get some blood, it injects malaria parasites into the person's bloodstream. The parasites travel to the liver, where they multiply,

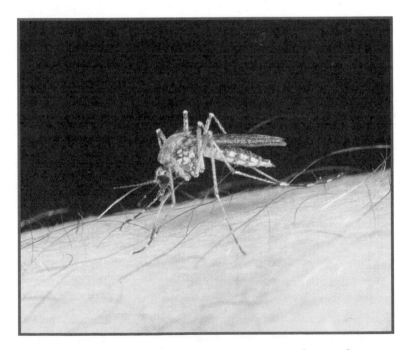

By biting humans, Anopheles *mosquitoes transmit malaria, a disease common in tropical regions.*

develop in stages, and invade the person's red blood cells. The person has now become a source of malaria. The next mosquito that bites the individual gets parasite-laden blood and will then infect the next person it bites.

People who have malaria are likely to have bouts of high fever, chills, and sweating. Malaria also causes anemia (a blood condition characterized by decreased numbers of red blood cells). When the disease is severe, it can affect the brain, kidneys, and other organs. People who live where malaria is common and are exposed to the disease repeatedly become immune, but the immunity does not last if they move to an environment where malaria rarely occurs.

Malaria cases are on the rise for several reasons.

- Although there are drugs to treat it, resistant strains of the parasite are increasing.
- More air travel to malaria-infested regions of the world has resulted in greater numbers of infected travelers, who take the disease home with them.
- Other factors, such as the movement of people into malarial zones, changes in rainfall patterns, and changes in the biting habits of mosquitoes have contributed to the spread of the disease.[6]

Scientists are trying to develop new drugs to which the parasites are not resistant. At present, no vaccine is available for the prevention of malaria, but researchers are experimenting with vaccines that interfere with biochemical processes in the parasite that are necessary for its survival and reproduction in a person's body. It is especially difficult to make vaccines that are effective against malaria. As the parasitic microbes go through different stages in their life cycle, they change in form and have different antigens. For this reason, immunity against one form of malaria does not lead to immunity against other forms. Researchers are working on making synthetic vaccines that string together antigen fragments from all four stages of microbial development.

Scientists are also working on vaccines that block the transmission of the parasites from infected humans to mosquitoes.[7]

Scientists are continually discovering and testing new and improved vaccines, using their increasing knowledge of the immune system. HIV, tuberculosis, and malaria are only a few of the many infectious diseases that researchers are studying in an effort to find new and better ways of protecting people from infection.

Alzheimer's Disease

Four million people in the United States have a progressive brain disorder known as Alzheimer's disease, which affects one in ten people over the age of 85. People with this devastating disease suffer from gradually worsening memory loss, inability to learn new information, problems in expressing themselves, confusion, loss of judgment, personality changes, and difficulty performing activities of daily living, such as cooking or balancing a checkbook. These problems worsen with time.

Consider the sad story of Janice, a lively, active grandmother who began to have disturbing memory lapses when she was 64. She often forgot to turn off the stove when she finished cooking, and she constantly misplaced things. Sometimes, she did not remember recent conversations with family or friends, and she forgot to keep appointments. Later, she had difficulty recognizing family members. She sometimes wandered away from home and didn't know how to get back. In addition, she could not remember that she had worked as an architect for many years.

Because Janice couldn't remember the right words, she had increasing difficulty expressing herself. She became more and more confused. At the end, she lost all ability to communicate, and she was totally dependent on others for her needs.

There may be a glimmer of hope for people who suffer from Alzheimer's disease. In experiments with mice, researchers have developed a vaccine that prevents the formation of amyloid plaques—deposits of protein in the brains of people with

Alzheimer's disease. This vaccine also clears away plaques that have already formed in the brains of the mice. It stimulates the mice to produce antibodies to the proteins in the plaque.[8]

Many problems must be solved before this research can be applied to people. There is no good way of measuring memory loss or intellectual capacity in mice, so it is difficult to measure whether the vaccine is actually effective in preventing changes in behavior. Although these mice had plaques, they did not develop "tangles"—knots of fibrous cells in their brains. Many researchers think that the "tangles" are the cause of the mental decline and that the plaques are by-products. In that case, dissolving the plaques in human brains might not reverse the symptoms of Alzheimer's disease.

Scientists are worried about the safety of using such a vaccine in humans. It might cause brain inflammation or trigger immune reactions against healthy tissues elsewhere in the body. The first step is to see if the vaccine is safe. Researchers are planning to conduct testing in a small number of people. If the vaccine has no toxic effects, then the next step would be to see if it works to reverse or prevent the mental degeneration associated with this terrible disorder.

Cancer

Cancer is a frightening word. Every year, about a million and a half people in the United States are diagnosed with some form of cancer. Although many people are treated successfully, there is still no sure cure for this feared killer. The tremendous efforts of scientists have led to the development of several anticancer drugs, and researchers have also experimented with vaccines to fight cancer. Cancer is actually many different diseases that affect many different organs in the body.

Normally, cells in the human body grow and reproduce in an orderly way. But cancer cells lack the controls that moderate the growth process, so they continue to multiply wildly. They compete with healthy cells for space and nutrients, and they may spread to distant parts of the body through the bloodstream or lymph channels.

There are differences between the usual vaccines against disease-causing organisms and cancer vaccines. First, a vaccine against an infectious disease such as polio produces an immune response that prevents a disease from occurring or makes it milder. A vaccine against cancer immunizes a person to stop the growth of the cancerous cells. Second, the familiar vaccines are made from antigens on microbes that the body's immune system recognizes as foreign. Normally, a person's immune system does not attack its own cells, so how can an anticancer vaccine work? Although cancer cells are the body's own cells, and not foreign, researchers have discovered that cancer cells produce antigens that are different from those on healthy cells. To mount an attack on the cancer cells, the immune system must recognize the cancer cells as foreign. Scientists have identified a large number of different antigens in prostate, breast, colon, lung, and ovarian cancers, as well as in lymphoma (cancer of the lymph glands) and melanoma (a serious form of skin cancer).

Scientists use several methods to generate anticancer antibodies. One method involves using cancer cells that have been removed from the person's body. Researchers treat the cells with adjuvants, which are special additives that boost an immune reaction, and then the mixture is ready for injection. The problem with this method is that a vaccine has to be made specially for each individual because each cancer is different. Other approaches involve the injection of various substances that increase the production of antigen by the tumor, or cancerous growth, which in turn increases the person's immune response.[9]

One group of researchers has been testing a vaccine against prostate cancer, using cancer cell antigens that were manufactured in the laboratory. They attached the antigens to a carrier molecule and injected the vaccine into mice. The mice produced antibodies to the cancer cell antigens. When the researchers tested the vaccine on men who had surgery for prostate cancer, the men also produced antibodies. The scientists hope that the vaccine may prevent the cancer from occurring again.[10]

Other researchers are testing different kinds of vaccines against melanoma. One vaccine is made from melanoma cells from different patients. These cells are grown in the laboratory, and a vaccine is made from a combination of antigens from the surface of the cancer cells. When people with melanoma were given the vaccine, they remained disease-free for more than twice as long as melanoma patients who did not receive the vaccine.[11]

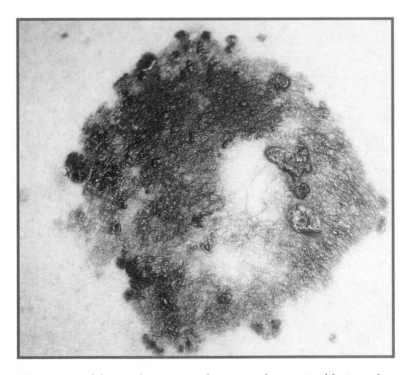

Skin cancer of the type known as melanoma is characterized by irregularities and changes in moles.

Cancer vaccines present many challenges. The cancer may suppress the immune system, so it might not produce antibodies in response to a vaccine. Tumors may be able to escape detection by the immune system, or they may kill immune system lymphocytes. Although anticancer vaccines may not be effective for advanced cancer, scientists believe they can help in the early stages of disease. There is one positive thing. Because the vaccine against hepatitis B helps reduce deaths from liver cancer, it has been called the first anticancer vaccine.

10

Vaccinations Around the World

IN THE LAST 150 years, the time required to travel completely around the world has decreased from 365 days to fewer than 3. Every day, 1.4 million people travel internationally by air. Many of them carry microbes that cause diseases, and they arrive at their destinations in less time than the incubation period for most infectious diseases.[1] Large movements of refugees and people who have families in one country but work in another country have spread new and emerging infections.

As an example, consider this scenario. After a boat trip on the Amazon River in Brazil, a man flew home to Switzerland. He felt fine when he got off the plane, but 10 days later he was dead. He had been bitten by the kind of mosquito that carries the tropical disease called yellow fever. This man had not received a vaccination for yellow fever before he left for his vacation, an action that could have saved his life.[2] The U.S. Institute of Medicine has estimated that an outbreak of yellow fever in a city such as New Orleans could result in as many as 100,000 cases of disease.[3]

Many diseases, such as HIV disease, malaria, tuberculosis, measles, pertussis, diphtheria, and hepatitis are easily carried and spread by travelers to many parts of the world. Vaccination of large numbers of people and prompt recognition of imported disease prevents epidemics.

Planes carry passengers to destinations around the globe. This departure board at Narita International Airport in Tokyo, which shows when planes are scheduled to leave and whether they are running on time, illustrates how distant parts of the world have become connected with each other.

Monitoring Disease Around the World

Reports of diseases that infect tourists traveling abroad appear on an Internet program called Program for Monitoring Infectious Diseases (ProMED-Mail), which is used by scientists, doctors, and other health-care professionals. This global electronic network for surveillance of infectious diseases collects information from 1,000 laboratory centers around the world in its efforts to warn people about outbreaks.

In today's world, where international travelers can be exposed to serious diseases and be back home before the end of the incubation period, ProMED-Mail plays an important role in protecting people from large epidemics. In addition to this, the WHO and Health Canada, which have joined to form the Global Public Health Information Network (GPHIN), provide reports from Pro-MED and other sources.

Information for Tourists

If you plan to travel to other countries, you should be protected from certain diseases by vaccinations a month or more in advance. In the case of hepatitis A, for example, you need a vaccination and booster in 6 to 12 months for complete protection. It takes weeks for immunity to develop.

If you plan to travel abroad as a civilian, you may be required to have vaccinations for a variety of diseases. Current information about what diseases are present in the countries you are visiting and what vaccinations you need can be obtained from your doctor or found through travel clinics. You can also get information from the CDC. Or you can find information on the Internet (see the To Find Out More section at the back of this book). You could also call your local clinic or health department to find out what shots you need.

When a vaccine is recommended, it means that a visitor to that country is at risk of exposure to disease. When a vaccine is required, a country does not want its own citizens to get the disease from you.

The Anthrax Situation

If you are a tourist, anthrax vaccination will not be on your schedule. However, if you are a member of the armed forces, you need to plan for it. Experts are concerned about the use of anthrax as a biological weapon. Anthrax is a disease caused by bacteria that

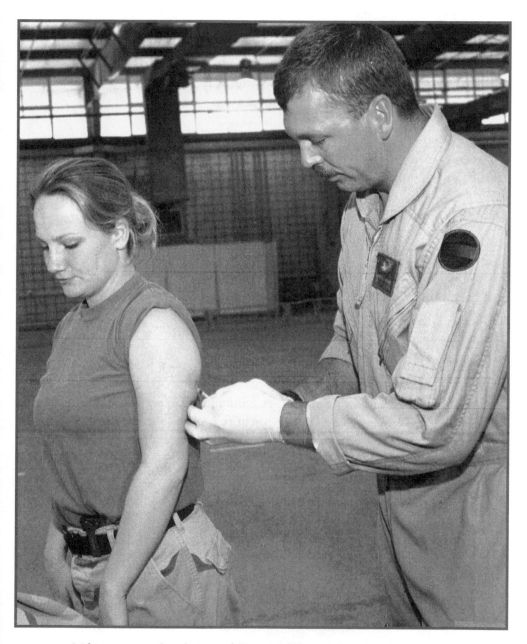

Military personnel in the United States are being vaccinated against anthrax. They may be exposed to the toxin produced by the anthrax bacteria.

begins with flulike symptoms. Within a week after its spores, or reproductive cells, are inhaled, victims are gasping for breath and almost always die. When anthrax spores are inhaled, anthrax is 99 percent lethal. In theory, 1 gram (0.02 ounce) of anthrax spores—about the weight of a paper clip—could kill 10 million people.[4]

In December 1997, U.S. Secretary of Defense William Cohen ordered all the nation's 2.4 million soldiers and sailors, including those on active duty, in the reserves, and in the National Guard, to receive anthrax vaccinations in the next 5 years. A relatively small number of individuals have resisted this effort to protect the nation's forces from biological warfare. They were willing to lose pay, be fined, be restricted to base or ship, or even be discharged from the military for refusing to be vaccinated.[5]

To people who question the safety of the anthrax vaccine, the Defense Department says that the vaccine has the approval of the FDA, has been used since 1970, and has an excellent safety record. However, critics of the anthrax vaccination program are concerned about possible side effects and think this vaccination should be voluntary.

Soon you may be able to get a vaccination against anthrax as an American citizen. Some experts in protection against terrorism are considering a program in which Americans may be offered shots against agents of biological warfare, including anthrax, in the not-so-distant future.[6]

Vaccination of Children Around the World

Richard and Marta Johnson adopted two children in Russia. The Russian authorities told them that the children had been given all their necessary vaccinations, but the Johnsons never received a written record. When the younger child developed whooping cough, they decided to have their own pediatrician check to see which vaccinations the children still needed. Their doctor gave them information about the diseases against which the children were immune, brought them up to date on those that were needed, and gave them information about what they needed in the future.

Although vaccinations for many diseases are reaching children in distant parts of the world, large numbers of children are not protected, especially in developing countries. For example, whooping cough and measles are still a major cause of death in children in some countries. And in March 1999, there was an outbreak of meningitis in Africa.

On March 8, 1999, people were streaming into clinics in Sudan. They wanted to be immunized against meningitis because an epidemic of the disease was spreading throughout the country. Although vaccination campaigns were underway in many areas, shortages of vaccine prevented many people from getting the necessary immunization. People who lived on the major roads were most exposed to the disease, because the roads put them in contact with many people who travel. In the most seriously affected areas, people started to panic. By May, when an international team had distributed 10.7 million doses of vaccine, 1,600 people had died.[7]

In another part of Africa, a woman named Sardi gives birth to a baby boy. She knows many children in Africa die from childhood diseases. To protect her child from the many diseases that are common in her village, she plans to go to a town 50 miles (80 kilometers) from where she lives to have her son vaccinated when he is a little older. She will have to walk there with her son on her back and then carry him home again.

Many vaccines that are taken for granted in the United States do not reach children in poor countries for 15 years after they are developed. In 1998, the Gates Children's Vaccination Program was introduced to speed the delivery of vaccines to children in developing countries. These vaccines protect against a group of respiratory, intestinal, and liver diseases, which take the lives of more than 2 million children a year worldwide.[8] The immunizations will probably save many millions of children

A doctor in India vaccinates people against cholera after a cyclone—a severe storm—contaminated their drinking water

from dying from preventable diseases. New vaccines, together with existing vaccines, may prevent 12 million deaths a year worldwide.[9]

The vaccination story will never end. New diseases will continue to appear and new vaccines will be found to prevent many of them.

Glossary

active immunity—immunity produced by the body in response to
stimulation by a disease-causing organism (naturally acquired
active immunity) or by a vaccine (artificially acquired active
immunity)

anthrax—a disease of sheep and cattle that can be transmitted to
humans

antibody—a protein molecule produced and secreted by B cells in
response to an antigen and capable of binding to that specific antigen

antigen—a substance that provokes an immune response

antitoxin—an antibody to a bacterial toxin

attenuated—weakened

B cell—a small white blood cell that is crucial to the immune
defenses. Also known as B lymphocytes, B cells are derived
from bone marrow (soft tissue located in the cavities of the
bones that is the source of all blood cells) and develop into
plasma cells, which produce antibodies.

booster—successive injection of a vaccine or revaccination to
boost immunity

conjugate vaccine—a vaccine in which proteins that are easily recognized by the immune system are linked to the outer coat
of a disease-causing microbe

culture—a group of cells or microorganisms grown in a laboratory

DNA—deoxyribonucleic acid; the genetic material in cells that contains the directions the cell uses to perform a particular function

epidemic—an outbreak of disease that spreads rapidly through a community

eradication—complete elimination; removal of all traces

gamma globulin—the part of the blood that contains a large percentage of the circulating antibodies

Haemophilus influenzae *type b (Hib)*—a bacterium that causes acute respiratory infections, including pneumonia, and other diseases, such as meningitis

hepatitis—inflammation of the liver, most often caused by different viruses that attack the liver

herpes zoster—shingles; a painful skin rash caused by the chickenpox virus

immunity—protection against infections

inactivated vaccine—vaccine made from a whole virus or bacterium that has no biological ability to grow or reproduce; a killed vaccine

incubation period—the time it takes for symptoms of a communicable disease to become apparent in someone who has been exposed to the disease

inoculation—the practice of giving an individual a weakened form of a disease to prevent development of a more dangerous strain. Inoculation was in use before the introduction of Jenner's vaccine against smallpox. Today, the words "inoculation" and "vaccination" are often used interchangeably.

live attenuated vaccine—a vaccine whose biological activity has not been inactivated, but whose ability to cause disease has been weakened

lymph—a transparent, slightly yellow fluid that carries lymphocytes, bathes the body tissues, and drains into the lymphatic vessels

lymph node—a small bean-shaped organ of the immune system, distributed widely throughout the body and linked by lymphatic vessels. Lymph nodes are gathering sites for B cells, T cells, and other immune cells.

lymphatic vessels—a body-wide network of channels similar to blood vessels that transport lymph to the immune organs and into the bloodstream

lymphocytes—small white blood cells that are produced in the bone marrow and thymus that are essential in immune defense

macrophage—a large and versatile white blood cell that acts as a microbe-devouring cell. It attacks invaders, and it also cleans up after invaders are destroyed.

memory cells—a subset of T cells and B cells that have been exposed to specific antigens and can then respond more readily when the immune system encounters the same antigens again

meningitis—inflammation of the lining of the spinal cord

microbe—a germ—small living organism, such as a bacterium or virus. Microbes can be helpful or harmful. They cannot be seen without a microscope.

mutate—to change a gene or unit of hereditary material that results in a new inheritable characteristic

naked DNA vaccine—a vaccine made up of deoxyribonucleic acid (DNA) that is not encased or encapsulated. In naked DNA vaccines, genetic material is injected directly into the vaccine recipient.

passive immunity—immunity resulting from the transfer of cells or antibodies or antiserum produced by another individual

patent—(verb) to obtain an exclusive right to make, use, or sell an invention

pertussis—whooping cough

pustule—a blister or pimple, particularly one containing pus

rabies—a contagious and fatal virus disease that can be transmitted to humans by dogs, raccoons, and other animals

recombinant genetic engineering—the technique by which genetic material from one organism is inserted into a foreign cell or another organism to produce the protein encoded by the inserted genes. (This method is also called recombinant DNA technology.)

rubella—German measles

shingles—a painful disease caused by the varicella-zoster virus, the same one that causes chickenpox

subunit vaccine—a vaccine that uses one or more components of a disease-causing microbe, rather than the whole microbe, to stimulate an immune response

T cell—a small white blood cell that is important in immune defenses. Also known as T lymphocytes, T cells mature in the thymus.

toxoid—an inactivated or killed organic toxin used to immunize against specific bacteria

varicella zoster—chickenpox

variolation—an outdated technique of immunization that involves inoculation of a person with material from a pustule of someone with smallpox

virulent—toxic, disease-causing

End Notes

Chapter 1

1. Wolfgang K. Joklik, "The Remaining Smallpox Stocks Are Too Valuable To Be Destroyed," *The Scientist,* 9 December 1996 (*http://www.the-scientist.library.upenn.edu/yr1996/dec/opin_961209.html*).
2. National Institute of Allergy and Infectious Diseases (NIAID), *Understanding Vaccines* (U.S. Department of Health and Human Services, National Institutes of Health [NIH] Publication No. 98–4219, January 1998), 2.
3. William Dudley, ed., *Epidemics: Opposing Viewpoints* (San Diego, CA: Greenhaven Press, 1999), 2.
4. Arno Karlen, *Man and Microbes* (New York: G. P. Putnam, 1955), 101–102.
5. NIAID, *Understanding Vaccines,* 1.
6. A. J. Harding Rains, *Edward Jenner and Vaccination* (East Sussex, England: Wayland Press, 1980), 50.
7. Karlen, *Man and Microbes,* 142.
8. "The First Recorded Smallpox Vaccination" (*http://home.sprynet.com/sprynet/~btomp/smallpox.htm*).
9. Edward Jenner, *Vaccination Against Smallpox* (New York: Prometheus Books, Great Mind Series, 1996).

10. Richard Gordon, *The Alarming History of Medicine* (New York: St. Martin's Griffin, 1997), 42–50.
11. Rains, *Edward Jenner,* 64.
12. Robert Desowitz, *The Thorn in the Starfish* (New York: W. W. Norton, 1987), 23–25.
13. James Cross Giblin, *When Plague Strikes* (New York: HarperCollins, 1995), 102.
14. Ibid.
15. Gilbin, 107.
16. Tim Beardsley, "Facing an Ill Wind," *Scientific American,* April 1999, 20.
17. Elizabeth Neus, "Smallpox Virus Faces Own Death," Gannet News Service, 26 May 1996 (*http://www.kadets.d20.co.edu/~lundberg/smallpox.html*).

Chapter 2

1. Paul A. Offit and Louis M. Bell, *What Every Parent Should Know About Vaccines* (New York: Macmillan, 1998), 4.
2. Desowitz, *Thorn in the Starfish,* 29.
3. Jenner, *Vaccination Against Smallpox,* 24–25.
4. NIAID, *Understanding Vaccines,* 8.
5. Henry Dreher, *The Immune Power Personality* (New York: Dutton, 1995), 39–40.

Chapter 3

1. "U.N. Seeks $500 Million to Meet Deadline for Eradicating Polio," *New York Times,* 12 July 1999.
2. Bonnie A. Maybury Okonek and Linda Morganstein, "Development of Polio Vaccines," (*http://www.accessexcellence.org/AE/AEC/CC/polio.html*).
3. Polio Information Center Online (*http://128.59.173.136/PICO/Chapters/History.html*).
4. Karlen, *Man and Microbes,* 150.

5. Karin Bellenir and Peter Dresser, eds., *Contagious and Non-Contagious Infectious Diseases* (Detroit: Omnigraphics, 1996), 192.
6. Ibid.
7. Philip Elmert-Dewett, "Reliving Polio," *Time*, 28 March 1994 (*http://www.pathfinder.com/time/magazine/archive/ 1994/940328/940328.health.html*).
8. Ibid.
9. "Jonas Salk, M.D., Interview" (*http://www.achievement.org/autodoc/page/sal0int-1*).
10. Polio.com, "Polio News" (*http://www.polio.com/nws_cam.htm*).
11. National Vaccine Information Center (*http://www.909shot.com/gnspolio.htm*).
12. Polio Information Center Online (*http://128.59.173.136/PICO/Chapters/Eradication.html*).
13. Centers for Disease Control and Prevention (CDC), "ACIP Vote Regarding Routine Childhood Polio Vaccinations Recommendations" (*http://www.cdc.gov/od/oc/media/pressrel/r990617.htm*)

Chapter 4

1. David Thomas, "Hepatitis C, the Silent Epidemic," *InteliHealth*, 3 September 1998, 1.
2. "Hepatitis A Outbreaks in the U.S. Are Target of Vaccine Campaign," *Wall Street Journal*, 12 November 1999, B1.
3. "Hepatitis A Vaccinations Urged for Children in 11 Western States," *New York Times*, 23 February 1999, F12.
4. Centers for Disease Control and Prevention (CDC), "Fact Sheet: Viral Hepatitis B" (*http://www.cdc.gov/ncidod/diseases/hepatitis/b/factvax.htm*).
5. "It's Worth a Shot," *Time*, 28 September 1998.
6. CDC, "Fact Sheet: Viral Hepatitis B."

7. Centers for Disease Control and Prevention (CDC), "General Information on Hepatitis B Vaccine" (*http://www.cdc.gov/nip/news/messhepb.htm*).

8. Immunization Action Council, IAC Express Report Number 50 (Alexandria, VA: Infectious Diseases Society of America, 26 January 1999), 3.

9. CDC, "Fact Sheet: Hepatitis B Vaccine

10. Ibid.

11. "Hepatitis C: How Widespread Is the Threat?" *New York Times,* 15 December 1998, F1.

12. Joanie Schrof, "New Help for Ailing Veterans," *U.S. News and World Report,* 8 February 1999, 67.

Chapter 5

1. Bellenir and Dresser, *Contagious and Non-Contagious Infectious Diseases,* 32–39.

2. Ibid.

3. Dudley, *Epidemics: Opposing Viewpoints,* 132.

4. Ibid.

5. Offit and Bell, *What Every Parent Should Know,* 39.

6. Ibid.

7. Ibid., 180.

8. National Foundation for Infectious Diseases, "Facts About Chickenpox for Adults" (*http://www.nfid.org/factsheets.varicellaadult.htm*).

9. Neal Halsey, "Parents Seem Chicken Over Chicken Pox Vaccine," *Johns Hopkins Health Insider,* November 1998.

10. Ibid., 1.

11. Infectious Diseases Society of America, *Information News,* 26 March 1999 (entire issue).

12. Lehigh Valley Hospital Health Network, "Measles: Infectious Diseases—Your Body and You" (*http://www.lvhhn.org/yourcare/body/m/measles.html*).

13. "Measles Outbreak Update" (Anchorage: State of Alaska Epidemiology Bulletin No. 21, 13 October 1998), 1.

14. Offit and Bell, *What Every Parent Should Know,* 69.
15. Ibid., 70–72.
16. Ibid., 57–58.
17. "Vaccination Nearly Ends Illness," *New York Times,* 27 November 1998, A31.
18. Tamar Lasky, Gina J. Terraciano, and Laurence Magder, et al., "The Guillain-Barré Syndrome and the 1992–1993 and 1993–1994 Influenza Vaccines," *New England Journal of Medicine* 339 (December 17 1998), 1797–1802.
19. "Front Line in Meningitis Campaign: Freshmen," *New York Times,* 2 November 1999, D1.

Chapter 6

1. "Immunization Roulette," *U.S. News and World Report,* 23 November 1998, 65.
2. Jamie Murphy, *What Every Parent Should Know About Childhood Immunization* (Boston: Earth Healing Products, 1993), 39–58.
3. Kathleen R. Stratton, Cynthia J. Howe, and Richard B. Johnston, Jr., eds., *Adverse Events Associated with Childhood Vaccines* (Washington, DC: National Academy Press, 1994), 275.
4. Centers for Disease Control and Prevention (CDC), "Vaccine Contamination Questions and Answers," (*http://www.cdc.gov/nip/vacsafe/contamfs.htm*).
5. Neil Z. Miller, *Vaccines: Are They Really Safe and Effective?* (Santa Fe, N.M.: New Atlantean Press, 1993), 50.
6. "SIDS, Sudden and Silent" (*http://kidshealth.org/cgi-bin/print_hit_bold.pl/parent/healthy/sids.html*).
7. Stratton, Howe, and Johnston, *Adverse Events Associated with Childhood Vaccines,* 109; Centers for Disease Control and Prevention (CDC), "What You May Have Heard About Vaccines . . . and What You Should Know" (*http://www.cdc.gov/nip/vacsafe/babysf2.htm*).

8. Centers for Disease Control and Prevention (CDC), "Multiple Sclerosis and Hepatitis B Vaccine" (*http://www.cdc.gov/nip/vacsafe/vaccinesafety/hottopics/ms.htm*).

9. Centers for Disease Control and Prevention (CDC), "General Information on Hepatitis B Vaccine" (*http://www.cdc.gov/nip/news/messhepb.htm*).

10. Murphy, *What Every Parent Should Know,* 88.

11. Centers for Disease Control and Prevention (CDC), "Six Common Misconceptions About Vaccines" (*http://cdc.gov/nip/publications/6mishome.htm*).

12. Stratton, Howe, and Johnston, *Adverse Events Associated with Childhood Vaccines,* 286.

13. Ibid., 1–4.

14. Ibid., 317–323.

Chapter 7

1. Stratton, Howe, and Johnston, *Adverse Events Associated with Childhood Vaccines,* 62.

2. Ibid., 65.

3. CDC, "Six Common Misconceptions," 6.

4. Ibid., 2.

5. Miller, *Vaccines,* 25.

6. Centers for Disease Control and Prevention (CDC), "What Would Happen If We Stopped Vaccinations?" (*http://www.cdc.gov/nip/vacsafe/valuefs.htm*).

7. *The Jordan Report 98: Accelerated Development of Vaccines* (Division of Microbiology and Infectious Disease, National Institute of Allergy and Infectious Diseases [NIAID], National Institutes of Health [NIH]), 42.

8. Ibid., 18.

9. CDC, "What Would Happen."

10. CDC, "What Would Happen."

11. CDC, "Six Common Misconceptions."

12. Ibid., 5.

13. *Vaccinate Adults!* 2, no. 2 (Fall/Winter 1998–1999).
14. CDC, "Six Common Misconceptions."
15. CDC, "What Would Happen."

Chapter 8

1. Geoffrey Cowley, "Vaccine Revolution," *Newsweek,* 27 July 1998, 48.
2. Carol Potera, "Making Needles Needless," *Technology Review,* September/October 1998, 69.
3. Centers for Disease Control and Prevention (CDC), "Rotavirus Fact Sheet" (*http://www.cdc.gov/nip/fs/Rotavirus.htm*).
4. Cowley, "Vaccine Revolution," 49.
5. "Cavity Vaccine," *Discover,* August 1998, 34.
6. NIAID, *Understanding Vaccines,* 20.
7. Cowley, "Vaccine Revolution," 49.
8. National Institute of Allergy and Infectious Diseases (NIAID), National Institutes of Health, (NIH), "Fact Sheet: Emerging Infectious Diseases" (*http://www.niaid.nih.gov/factsheets/eid.htm*).
9. CDC, "What Would Happen."
10. "Vaccine Revolution," 49.
11. NIAID, *Understanding Vaccines,* 27.
12. NIAID, "Fact Sheet: Emerging Infectious Diseases."
13. David B. Weiner and Robert C. Kennedy, "Genetic Vaccines," *Scientific American,* July 1999, 50 (*http://www.sciam.com/1999/0799weiner.html*).

Chapter 9

1. National Institute of Allergy and Infectious Diseases (NIAID), National Institutes of Health (NIH), "Fact Sheet: Challenges in Designing HIV Vaccines" (*http://www.niaid.nih.gov.factsheets/challvacc.htm*).

2. David Baltimore and Carole Heilman, "HIV Vaccines: Prospects and Challenges," *Scientific American,* July 1998, 103.

3. Ibid.

4. National Institute of Allergy and Infectious Diseases (NIAID), National Institutes of Health (NIH), "Fact Sheet: Tuberculosis," (*http://www.niaid.nih.gov.factsheets/tb.htm*).

5. *Jordan Report,* 76.

6. Thomas C. Nchinda, "Malaria: A Reemerging Disease in Africa," *Emerging Infectious Diseases,* 4 (no. 3) July–September 1998 (*http://www.cdc.gov/ncidod/EID/vol4no3/nchinda.htm*).

7. National Institute of Allergy and Infectious Disease (NIAID), National Institutes of Health (NIH), "Fact Sheet: Malaria Research" (*http://www.niaid.nih.gov/factsheets/Malaria2.htm*).

8. Geoffrey Cowley, "Outsmarting Alzheimer's," *Newsweek,* 19 July 1999, 59.

9. *Jordan Report,* 83–87.

10. Intelihealth: Johns Hopkins Health Information, (*http://www.intelihealth.com/IH/ihtIH?t=333&st+333&r=E MIHC000&c=202374*).

11. "Melanoma Vaccine Program Shows Promise," *NYU Physician,* 52 (no. 1) spring 1999, 14–15.

Chapter 10

1. Centers for Disease Control and Prevention (CDC), "Travelers' Health" (*http://www.cdc.gov/ncidod/EID/vol4no3/cetron.htm*).

2. Gary Taubes, "Virus Hunting on the Web," *Technology Review,* November/December 1998, 51–55.

3. Kenneth R. Foster, et al., "The Philadelphia Yellow Fever Epidemic of 1793," *Scientific American,* August 1997, 93.

4. "The Weapon Too Terrible for the Parade of Horribles," *New York Times,* 8 February 1998.

5. "A Vaccination War Erupts in Military," *Christian Science Monitor,* 28 January 1999.

6. "Launching a Homeland Defense," *Christian Science Monitor,* 29 January 1999.

7. Communicable Disease Surveillance and Response (*http://www.who.int/emc/outbreak_news/n1999/may/n12amay1999.html*).

8. "A Kinder Gentler Bill," *Newsweek,* 14 December 1998, 57.

9. Cowley, "Vaccine Revolution," 48.

To Find Out More

Books

Biddle, Wayne. *A Field Guide to Germs.* New York: Henry Holt, 1995.

Burge, Michael C., and Don Nardo. *Vaccines: Preventing Disease.* San Diego, CA: Lucent Books, 1992.

Freidlander, Mark P., Jr., and Terry M. Phillips. *The Immune System: Your Body's Disease Fighting Army.* Minneapolis: Lerner, 1998.

Hyde, Margaret O. *Know About Tuberculosis.* New York: Walker, 1994.

Hyde, Margaret O., and Elizabeth H. Forsyth. *AIDS: What Does It Mean To You?* New York: Walker, 1996.

Hyde, Margaret O., and Elizabeth H. Forsyth. *The Disease Book.* New York: Walker, 1997.

Kehret, Peg. *The Year I Got Polio.* Morton Grove, IL: Albert Whitman, 1996.

National Institute of Allergy and Infectious Diseases (NIAID), *Understanding Vaccines.* Bethesda, MD: National Institutes of Health (NIH), 1998.

Rains, A.J. Harding. *Edward Jenner and Vaccination.* East Sussex, England: Wayland, 1980.

Scientific American Special Issue. *Life, Death and the Immune System.* New York: W.W. Freeman, 1994.

Silverstein, Alvin and Virginia. *Measles and Rubella.* Springfield, NJ: Enlsow, 1997.

Silverstein, Alvin, and Virginia and Laura Silverstein Nunn. *Hepatitis.* Springfield, NJ: Enslow, 1994.

Veggeberg, Scott. *Lyme Disease.* Springfield, NJ: Enslow, 1998.

Organizations and Online Sites

American Liver Foundation
75 Maiden Lane, Suite 603
New York, NY 10038
http://www.liverfoundation.org
A national organization that provides information about liver diseases.

Centers for Disease Control and Prevention (CDC)
1600 Clifton Road
Atlanta, GA 30333

Specific CDC web sites:
http://www.cdc.gov/nip
National Immunization Program, which provides information on new vaccines, current issues such as hepatitis B and global polio eradication, and rotavirus vaccination.

http://www.cdc.gov/ncidod/diseases/hepatitis/hepatitis.htm
An online source of information about hepatitis.

http://www.cdc.gov/travel
An online source of travel information that tells about disease outbreaks, recommended vaccines for travelers, and current issues concerning travelers' health. It provides reference material for international travelers.

http://www.cdc.gov/travel/hepa_ig.htm
An online source of information for travelers who need specific information about hepatitis B.

Immunization Action Coalition and the Hepatitis B Coalition
1573 Selby Avenue
St. Paul, MN 55104
http://www.immunize.org
A source of educational materials about childhood, adolescent, and adult immunization, as well as hepatitis B.

Infectious Diseases Society of America
National Immunization Information Network
99 Canal Center Plaza, Suite 210
Alexandria, VA 22314
http://www.idsociety.org/vaccine/index/html
A source of information about scientists' commitment to vaccination and the usefulness of vaccines in the prevention of disease.

National Coalition for Adult Immunization
4733 Bethesda Avenue, Suite 750
Bethesda, MD 20814
http://www.medscape.com/NCAI
A source of information about publications and immunization schedules concerning adult immunization.

National Vaccine Information Center (NVIC)
(former name: Dissatisfied Parents Together)
512 West Maple Avenue, Suite 206
Vienna, VA 22180
http://www.909shot.com
Provides information about diseases and the vaccines designed to prevent them as well as how to report vaccine-associated reactions.

World Health Organization (WHO)
Regional Office for the Americas/
Pan American Health Organization
525 23rd Street NW
Washington, DC 20037
http://www.who.int/gpv
A source of information on health topics that affect people around the world, including many vaccine-preventable diseases.

Index

Iron lung, 27–29, *28*

Jenner, Edward, 13–14, *14*
Jesty, Benjamin, 13
Johnson, Arkesha, 38

Liver cancer, 37, 39, 99
Lyme disease, 83, *83*

Ma, Julian, 81
Making vaccines, 81–84
Malaria, 80-81, 92–95, *93*
Mantoux test, 90
Mather, Cotton, 11
MDR-TB, 92
Measles, 17, 23, 49–50, *49*, 57,
  66, 72, 105
Meister, Joseph, 18
Memory cells, 21–22
Meningitis, 52-53, 55–56, 82,
  105
Mercury, 59–60
Military, 102–104, *103*
Milkmaids, 12–13
Miscarriage, and mumps, 52
MMR (measles, mumps, and
  rubella) vaccine, 49–52, *51*, 57
Monitoring
  adverse reactions, 66–68
  diseases, 101–102
Montagu, Mary Wortley, 9-11,
  10
Mosquitoes, 93–94, *93*
MS (multiple sclerosis), 64–65
Mumps, 49, 50-52, *51*, 57, 66

type of vaccine, 23
Nasal spray vaccines, 77, 78

Oral vaccines, 23, 32, 75, 78, 79,
  79, 80–81

Passive immunity, 22
Pasteur, Louis, 18, *19*
Pertussis (whopping cough), 17,
  42, 46–47, 58, 66, 73–74,
  104-105
Phipps, James, 13, *14*
Pneumococcal vaccine, 57
Polio, 17, 25–34, *28*, 66
  contaminated vaccines, 61–62
  eradication of, 32-33, *33*
  history of, 26–27, *26*
  how it spreads, 25
  oral vaccine, 23, *31*, 32, 75, 78,
    79
  Salk vaccine, 31–32, *31*
  what causes polio, 25
Positive skin test, 90
Postpolio syndrome, 26
Pregnancy, 23, 52
ProMED-Mail (Program for
  Monitoring Infectious Dis-
  eases), 101–102

Rabies, 18, *19*, 84
Ramses V, 8, *9*
Recombinant genetic engineering,
  81
Recommended immunizations,
  57

About the Authors

MARGARET O. HYDE is the author of almost eighty books for young people, many devoted to topics of science and health or concerned with important social issues. Her books for Franklin Watts include *Missing and Murdered Children* and *When the Brain Dies First* (written with John F. Setaro, M.D.). She has also written a number of documentary programs for television. She lives in Essex, Connecticut.

ELIZABETH H. FORSYTH, M.D., is a psychiatrist who has written seventeen books in collaboration with Margaret O. Hyde, concerning such subjects as AIDS, asthma, mental illness, homosexuality, violence, and sexual abuse. She lives in Phoenix, Arizona, with her husband, Ben R. Forsyth, M.D.